James Greenwood

Sketches of Society and Travel

James Greenwood

Sketches of Society and Travel

ISBN/EAN: 9783337292416

Printed in Europe, USA, Canada, Australia, Japan

Cover: Foto ©Andreas Hilbeck / pixelio.de

More available books at **www.hansebooks.com**

"Sure to be somebody nice, Charlie thinks, or it would not be worth a seven miles drive in the wet."

"His expectations are scarcely realized."

SOCIAL PROBLEMS.

SKETCHES OF SOCIETY AND TRAVEL.

BY AN "AMATEUR CASUAL," AND OTHERS.

WITH ILLUSTRATIONS.

NEW YORK:
PUBLISHED BY HURD AND HOUGHTON,
459 BROOME STREET.
1868.

CONTENTS.

Frontispiece. — "Social Problems." Drawn by G. Bowers.
Something about Breakfast 1
An Evening with my Uncle 5
Twenty-four Hours of the Season . . . 12
    (With a double-page illustration by Florence Claxton.)
Engaged! 14
Humours of the Paris Exhibition . . . 19
St. Valentine's Day 29
    (With an illustration by Florence and Adelaide Claxton.)
Canine Celebrities 36
The Private Life of a Public Nuisance . . 46
Modern Beau-Brummelism 57
Balls in Vienna 65
Recollections of a Bachelor 71
A Week in a Country House 79
What's in the Papers? 98
Upstairs and down 102

SKETCHES OF SOCIETY AND TRAVEL.

SOMETHING ABOUT BREAKFAST

IT has often been asserted that as long as human beings congregate together like wild beasts at 'feeding times,' this age has no right to lay claim to superior civilization, and that it would be an improved manner of life if relays of food could be brought to some particular place at stated times, to which any who chose might resort.

As it is an acknowledged fact, that society and conversation are the best promoters of digestion, the plan that these captious people propose would be both unwholesome and unsocial, but it might be advantageously acted upon in the matter of breakfast, for that, as English people ordain it, is decidedly a mistake.

'Breakfast is such a charmingly social meal,' we heard a lady once say in speaking of a large breakfast in a country-house, 'every one comes down so fresh, everybody is in time, and ready for the duties and pleasures of the day. I consider it a delightful moment.' It was a sentimental and poetical view, but as far as possible removed from the truth; for in our estimation it is a peculiarly unhappy moment, and one in which many persons are prone to regard their fellow-creatures as their natural enemies.

When people are hungry and cold it follows as a matter of course that they are cross, and as large parties in country-houses usually occur in the winter, this is tolerably sure to be the case. Shy people, too, are always shy in the morning; they cannot take up life where they left it the night before, or say 'Good-morning' at all in the same happy and friendly spirit in which they said 'Good-night.'

People are not ready for social intercourse till they have been up at least three hours. It is quite curious to see how disagreeable really good-humoured people often are before breakfast. They are often conscious of their moroseness, and try to conceal it by utter silence or cynical smiles; but with all their endeavours we are aware that it would be a service of danger to speak to them, and whether it be our most valued friend, or simply a highly agreeable or intellectual acquaintance, we equally hope that it may never be our fate to meet him again at breakfast. Surely it would be a great advantage to the world if these individuals breakfasted alone!

Perhaps the most depressing thing we can meet with is anything like hilarity or even great cheerfulness so early in the day. Few things are more trying than the jovial, hearty manner in which the master of the house often enters the room where his guests are assembled in the morning. If in winter, with blue nose and red hands, loud in his praise of the weather (which to our thinking is simply detestable), advising every one to follow his example and take a turn before breakfast: 'Sharpens the appetite; freshens one up; does a world of good.' Take a turn before breakfast that raw January day! you cannot even reply except by drawing closer to the fire, and looking with horror at the freezing fog through the window. You sit down to breakfast to endure another trial from your well-meaning host, he being one of those who invariably make a programme of the day for other people, totally regardless of the fact that what people may like to do at two o'clock they dislike at ten, and vice versâ. But all this goes for nothing with your cheerful friend. He usually calls to his wife, who is absorbed in a tea-pot at the farthest end of the table, ' Well, my dear, and what have you arranged for our friends to do to-day?' There is a murmured response to the effect that no one wishes to do anything. ' It is so very cold to-day,' Mrs. —— replies, languidly.

' Cold! not at all; that is so like you ladies, who never take any exercise, and do nothing to promote circulation; then you say it is cold! It is a fine, healthy, seasonable day; no sign of rain or snow. A day like this in January must not be wasted. Come, what will you all do? What would you like?'

' To be left alone,' is the unspoken reply in the mind of most of his guests, but of course the ungracious thought is not put into words. The pertinacious pleasure-hunter maps out the day for them. They can only resign themselves to his will, hoping that some happy coincidence, such as morning visitors, or a fall of snow, may give them a pretext for remaining comfortably by the fireside.

There are always some people who are more restless or less self-sufficing than others, who really prefer anything to their own society or remaining quiet; .but these are exceptions, and to those who are victims to this kind of energetic ruling it is poor comfort to know that the same wearisome repetition awaits them on the morrow.

Kind-hearted people often unintentionally inflict considerable annoyance on their friends by inquiring anxiously every morning after their health. One comfort is that the inquirer often forgets to wait for a reply; for as sleepless nights and aching heads are in themselves sufficiently miserable, few are desirous of going through a cross-examination upon them.

There has been a considerable change of late years in the fashion of breakfast. It is a good deal more *ad libitum* as to time, ranging from half-past nine to twelve. Tea and coffee are seldom now put upon the table, but are made out of the room, or by servants, on the side-table, who hand the cups as they are wanted. In some large houses several small tables are set for breakfast, so that, as there are only three, or at most four places, people may be said in some sense to breakfast alone, or at least with whom they please. This is, upon the whole, a good arrangement, but we doubt if it would not be still more desirable for people to breakfast alone in their rooms. The objection to this would probably be, that to carry up breakfast to eighteen or twenty people as varied and *recherché* as it is made now, consisting of fish, hot and cold meat, and fruit, as well as tea, coffee, bread, butter, and eggs—to send up, in fact, to each person a miniature dinner, would exhaust the resources of the largest establishment. One way, and perhaps the best way of meeting this difficulty would be to imitate the example of most foreigners, who have a cup of coffee or chocolate when they first rise, and only come down at eleven or twelve o'clock for the *déjeûner*, which with them corresponds to our luncheon; for no more eating is considered necessary till dinner-time, which is generally not later than seven o'clock. They have meat and wine as well as tea and coffee, and their *déjeûner*, in fact, combines breakfast and luncheon in one. This is in many respects a much wiser division of the day, as it leaves the whole afternoon free for exercise or amusement, either at home or abroad. But the amount of food that is put before us at breakfast is totally unnecessary, and if the meal were changed to a more simple one there would be no longer any difficulty about having it alone.

Though we have been discussing our breakfast, nothing has been said of the food of which it should consist. People's tastes are so different that it is quite impossible to lay down any gastronomic law upon a meal the constituents of which vary from bread and water, to salmon and grouse, and *pâté de foie gras*. We have seen unhappy wretches deliberately pour out a tumbler of cold water as their only breakfast beverage. Others, who make equal sacrifices at the shrine of health, are content to abjure even bread and butter, and breakfast entirely on some unpalateable mess, which, by dint of advertisements, has worked its way into fashion. Gentlemen who are addicted to field sports, and who for the most part despise luncheon, make breakfast a most substantial meal. Indeed, modern breakfasts seem drifting back to the beef and ale and goodly capons that young ladies found necessary to support nature in Queen Elizabeth's time. Ladies, and idle men of a more sedentary turn, are contented to depend mainly upon luncheon.

There are other kinds of breakfasts, besides the early morning meal of which we have been speaking. It is a constant habit with the literary world in London to have *réunions* of scientific and agreeable people early in the day, and what in the evening would be a *conversazione*, in the morning is simply called a breakfast. But the greatest misnomer of all is the habit, in London, of calling a dinner, and a ball and a supper, if given *al fresco*, a 'breakfast.' No one dreams of going to these parties till five o'clock, and they last frequently till the small hours of the morning. As the meeting usually takes place in the garden or grounds of some villa near London, the guests appear in morning dresses, which we suppose is the reason of this strangely misapplied term.

There is another annoyance to which those who never breakfast alone are exposed. Letters in the country always arrive in the morning, and we are tolerably sure that when we go down stairs to find a packet of letters on the table awaiting us. It is amusing to watch the different manner in which people behave about their letters. Some dart eagerly upon them, are instantly absorbed in their contents, from time to time doling out small pieces of intelligence from them; others examine them carefully, and then lay them aside, deferring the pleasure or the pain of their perusal to a 'more convenient season;' others, and these for the most part young men, take them up with real or affected indifference, and transfer them at once to their pockets. The chances are that these consist principally of reminders, more or less pressing, from the neighbourhood of Bond Street, Regent Street, and Piccadilly. Their contents may possibly be paraphrased in the parody of a well-known ballad:—

'You remember, you remember,
    The little bill you owe;
'Tis but two pound ten and four, sir,
    And I've waited long, you know.

'On my word, sir, on my word, sir,
    I wouldn't trouble now,
But I've got a long account, sir,
    To make up, and don't know how.

'You do take, sir, you do give, sir,
    Three letters every day;
O D V is what you take, sir,
    I O U is what you pay.'

It is to be feared that these 'rejected addresses' form a large portion of many people's correspondence! There is one very odd peculiarity that many people have about their letters, and one for which it is difficult to account. If a letter or note is brought, and the receiver is somewhat puzzled to know from whence it comes, the seal is closely investigated, the direction pondered over, the postmark held up to the light; every possible trouble is taken to examine the outside of a letter, when, by simply opening it, the desired knowledge would be attained. Does this show that human nature delights in a mystery?

In some houses it is the custom for the children to be brought down to be admired at breakfast. This habit, unless the children are quiet to stupidity, cannot fail to be a nuisance. The only time that we can gladly hail the appearance of children out of their own legitimate sphere, is in the formidable half-hour before dinner is announced. Then they create a diversion, and possibly suggest topics of conversation.

Breakfast is generally, more or less, a solemn process. The only aim at sprightliness it was ever our fate to witness was so disastrous in its results that we could only hope the attempt would never be repeated. It was at a large party in a country-house, and the conversation had accidentally turned upon eggs. The young lady of the house, who was seated by a *ci-devant jeune homme*, an exquisite of the last generation, who had been evidently taken with her beauty and gay spirits, declared that it was impossible to break an egg by pressing it ever so tightly, provided you held it in such a manner that the two ends, and no other part, touch the palms of the hands. Her neighbour heard her with a supercilious smile, and recommended her to try. She repeated that she had seen it done constantly, and would convince him there and then of the truth of her assertion. So saying, she took up an egg, and turning towards him, said, ' Now, see if I am not right!' When, to her dismay, the egg smashed at once, and its contents spurted over the very particular gentleman by her side, soiling his faultless shirt and waistcoat, and clinging pertinaciously to his whiskers and stubbly beard. Utterly dismayed at such a very unexpected disaster, partly from amusement, and partly from nervousness, Miss —— burst into a violent fit of laughing. Her example was followed by several others, for in truth nothing could present a more ludicrous and unhappy appearance than the poor man. Besides which, he was furiously angry, believing the whole thing to have been a previously arranged practical joke, and to see that he was the laughing-stock of the company, of course enraged him still more. In vain the poor girl tried to explain that the accident was quite unintentional, and, indeed, that her theory still held good, as the egg was broken not by the pressure but by her ring, which she had forgotten to remove. He would hear nothing, hurried out of the room to repair the mischief done to his dress, and would not return to the breakfast-table; in fact, we did not see him again, for he left the house the same day.

We have not spoken of the arrangement of a breakfast-table, or the pretty decorations of which it is capable. Flowers seem more in keeping with breakfast than with dinner, for if the china is ever so beautiful, or the damask ever so fine, a breakfast-table is dull and colourless without them. But however inviting it may be made, we still hold to our theory that for the most part it is better to breakfast alone.

AN EVENING WITH MY UNCLE.

HOW I first came to know Uncle Gawler, how it happened that our acquaintance, at first of the simplest sort, ripened gradually to a friendship warm and durable, need not be here discussed. It is sufficient for the purposes of this paper to state that between my uncle and myself such a happy condition of affairs prevails. The act of parliament which regulates the times and seasons during which my uncle may transact business with his numerous other poor relations in no way affects me; indeed it is more often 'after seven' than before that I make my calls, and I am always welcome. The strong spring-bolt that secures the flap-door of my uncle's shop counter is cheerfully withdrawn at my approach, giving me free access to the sanctum beyond—where the money-till with its silver 'well,' as large as a washing-bowl, and its gold 'well,' bigger than a quart basin, is always ajar; where on back counters, and shelves, and bunks are strewn rings, and pins, and brooches, and lockets, and bracelets (all solid and good gold, as attested by the grim glass bottle labelled 'aquafortis,' conveniently perched on its little bracket), where deep drawers, open just a little, reveal countless tiny and precious packets, done up in brown paper, and white paper, and stout bits of rag, and patched with a blue, or a red, or a yellow ticket, to indicate the number of pounds sterling that have been advanced on them; where watches, gold and silver, lie heaped together in a living heap, as one may say, each one hobbled to a pawn ticket, and left to die, but not yet dead, but, faithful in the discharge of its duty, clamorously 'tick, tick, ticking,' though nobody now takes the least interest in its time-keeping, nor minds its urgent whispering of the flight of time any more than the angler minds the gasping of the fish he has just landed. Were I a sentimental writer (which, thank goodness, I am not), and this a sentimental article, I have no doubt that a very pretty paragraph might be written on these faithful little monitors consigned to dungeon darkness and the stillness of death for just so long a time as may suit the convenience of the tyrant man. Torn from the bosom where they had so long lain nestling; abandoned by the hand that gave them life and motion, there they lie, true even unto death, the uncompromising, though somewhat astonished 'tick, tick' of the English lever; the plethoric and muffled tones of the old-fashioned 'hunter' of the mechanic; the spasmodic whimpering of the wretched Genoese, reminding one of—of— (not being ready with a happy simile I turn to Mr. Gawler, who is churchwarden, and who promptly suggests) cases of desertion on doorsteps.

It must not, however, be inferred from the above statement of the wealth in my Uncle Gawler's possession that he is as well-to-do in the world as many other of my relations in the same degree. He is not, for instance, as rich as my Uncle Attenborough, whose meanest place of business is a palace compared with that in which my poorer uncle carries on his trade. Uncle Attenborough affects plate glass and green and gold ornamentation, and informs you, through the medium of off-hand little notice-boards in his window, what is his price—per peck—for pearls and diamonds, and what he can give, per ton, for Australian bullion. Should the keeper of the crown jewels call on Uncle Attenborough, and request the fullest possible advance on them, he would no doubt be packed off with a satisfactory 'ticket.'

Such matters, however, are altogether above Uncle Gawler. He makes no pretension to dealing in diamonds, or foreign bullion, or sculpture or paintings by the old masters. It is a wonder, considering the locality in which his business is carried on—near Whitecross Street, St. Luke's—that so much valuable property is confided to his keeping; and, doubtless, the fact is mainly due—firstly, to the great number of years he has been established; and, secondly, to the convenient arrangement of his premises. It is a corner house, and the shop, which faces the High Street, is an innocent jeweller's shop, and nothing more. There are neatly-written cards in the window, variously inscribed, 'jewellery repaired,' 'watch glasses fitted,' 'ladies' ears pierced,' &c.; so that even though one should happen to be seen entering Mr. Gawler's shop,—nay, even though an inquisitive brute should be mean enough to spy from outside, and see one hand his 'Dent' to Mr. Gawler, and receive in exchange for it a neatly-folded bit of pasteboard, the evidence of the pawning would be anything but complete; watch glasses will come to grief, and watch works need repair, and it is the commonest thing in the world for the watchmaker to give the owner a memorandum, as security for his property. I have known fellows in the Strand take the 'Angel' omnibus on purpose to avail themselves of the services of Mr. Gawler.

But it is not on watch and jewel and trinket-pawners that Mr. Gawler relies for the support of his business. The street, of which my uncle's shop forms the corner, is one of the most densely populated streets in London. It is a market street, a street of shops, abounding in 'courts,' and 'alleys,' and 'yards,' with entrances like accidental chinks in the wall, and swarming with men, and women, and children, as rats swarm in a sewer. It is a roaring street for business; there are twenty-two butchers' shops in it, seventeen bakers' shops, and twenty-seven gin shops and beer shops. So it may easily be imagined that Uncle Gawler does his share of trade.

He is well prepared for it. Up the street by the side of the innocent-looking jeweller's shop—a longish way up the street—is a mean-looking doorway, that might be the entrance to a back yard. That it is something more than this, however, may be at once perceived by the stone threshold worn through to the bricks beneath, and the doorpost paint-rubbed and grimy of elbow grease. This is the poor pawners' entrance. It opens on to a passage, extending down the whole length of which is a row of latched doors, close together and hinge to hinge. There are eleven of these doors, and they belong to as many 'boxes' or compartments about four feet wide and ten deep, boarded on each side, and with a portion of counter (boarded, of course, from the top downwards) in front. There is a little bolt on the inside of the cell door, so that if a customer desires privacy he can secure himself from observation until his negotiation with the pawnbroker is completed. This precaution is—at least as regards the daytime—quite superfluous; for when the door is closed, the closet is dark as evening, making it next to impossible for any one to recognise his neighbour, except by the sound of his voice. I have said that each closet is fronted by a portion of the long counter which extends from one end of the pawning compartment to the other—I should rather have said that it is a ledge raised a foot above the level counter that faces the customer, the said raised ledge being, doubtless, intended as a check against the evil disposed, who might be tempted to advantage themselves of the bustle of much business, and walk off with their own or their neighbours' unransomed goods.

Against the wall opposite to the boxes, and facing the middle one, the 'spout' is built. The 'spout' at a pawnbroker's, as the gentle reader will please to understand, is a boxed-in space penetrating the upper warehouse floors, and contrived for the more ready delivery of pledged goods; which consisting, as they usually do among poor folks, of wearing apparel, and boots, and shoes, and bed-linen, may be collected from their various places of stowage and bundled by the dozen through the aperture in question from the top of the house to the bottom. To accommodate Uncle Gawler's extensive business, his 'spout' was of enormous size. The opening was as large as a kitchen chimney, and to two sides of it upright ladders were fixed.

Astraddle over the hole on the top floor was a windlass with a stout rope and a chain and a couple of hooks depending from it. This was used to wind up the sacksfull of pledged bundles, and no doubt saved a vast amount of labour. About the spare spaces (very few) of Uncle Gawler's shop walls were stuck various placards and business notices: one relating to the rates of interest allowed by law; one or two relating to recent instances of prosecution, and conviction, of persons pawning the property of others without their permission, and of other persons who had endeavoured to foist upon the unsuspecting pawnbroker 'Brummagem' ware, reputed to be honest gold or silver. There were other placards more or less curious, but none more so than one which in red and conspicuous letters, bore the mysterious announcement that 'there could be no parting after eleven o'clock.' A solution, however, to this mystery, and many others, appeared in the course of the evening I passed with Uncle Gawler.

How I came to enjoy that rare privilege I will explain in a few words. Although my calls at the shop in St. Luke's were not unfrequent, they had invariably taken place on some other day than Saturday. It was a real pleasure to call and see Uncle Gawler: he was always so filled with contentment and gratitude. 'How was he getting on?' 'Oh, nicely, thanky—very nicely; a little overdone with work, that's all: small cause for complaint you think, eh, young fellow? Ah! but the amount of business to be attended to in this place is enormous, sir—en-normous!' And then he would cast his eyes towards the long row of 'boxes,' and from them to the mighty 'spout,' with the cable and the chain and hooks dangling down, and sigh a pleasant sigh, and jingle the keys in his pocket.

He said this, or something very like, so often, that one could not help looking about him for symptoms of the enormous business Uncle Gawler made so much of. Looking about for these symptoms he failed to discover them. Although there was kept up a pretty constant slamming of the box-doors, and a briskish clamour of 'serve me, please,' 'it's my turn,' and 'ain't that there come down yet?' the eleven boxes were never a quarter filled, and never at any time had I dropped in at such a time of pressure that Mr. Gawler was unable to tuck his hands under his coat-tails and gossip for half an hour, while his two young men plodded along, the one examining and valuing articles brought to pawn, and the other making out the deposit-tickets and handing over the money, but with very little show of excitement. This circumstance, coupled with another, viz., that Uncle Gawler was invariably as unruffled as regards his habiliments as though he had just dressed for an evening party, drove me to the conclusion that either the worthy old gentleman possessed a marvellous aptitude for getting through an 'enormous amount' of business with perfect ease, or else that he was slightly given to exaggeration. At last came the eventful evening when my unworthy suspicions were vanquished, and my belief in Uncle Gawler established more firmly than ever.

It was a Saturday evening and the time of year was July. I had not met Uncle Gawler for several days, and it happening that a friend had kindly given me an order for the admission for two on the Adelphi Theatre, I thought it would be a good opportunity for a manifestation of my regard for him. It was rather late, 'but,' thought I, 'he is sure to be ready dressed, and he will only have to pop on his hat and we may be off at once.' Entering Uncle Gawler's shop I was immediately struck with astonishment, not to say awe. The two young men were there—Uncle Gawler was there, but how changed! No longer was he an elderly gentleman dressed for an evening party, but a person whose avocation it was to put down mob risings, to quell riots, to stop prize-fights, and who, calmly confident, expected each moment to be called on. It was his custom to wear a black satin stock and a diamond pin; these were cast aside, and, only for the neck-band of his shirt, his throat was bare. Ever before I had seen him in a coat of the glossiest black; now he wore no coat at all, but a waistcoat with tight black holland sleeves, like a porter at a paper-warehouse. Usually he was particular as to the arrangement of his hair, so that the side-pieces were cunningly coaxed upwards to conceal the nakedness of his crown; this, however, was no time for an indulgence of such weaknesses, and his stubbly, iron-grey locks appeared in the same state of delightful confusion they were originally thrown into by the bath-towel.

Whatever was Mr. Gawler's object, it was evident at a glance that both his young men were prepared to second him while breath remained in their bodies. Like their master, they had thrown aside their neckerchief, but, unlike him, they were without black holland sleeves to their waistcoats, and wore their shirt-sleeves rolled back above their elbows. And all for what? Never before had I found Uncle Gawler's shop so peaceful. With the exception of one, the eleven boxes were quite empty, and the exception was provided in a shape no more formidable than that of a young laundress, who was redeeming a brace of flat irons, and mildly remonstrating with Mr. Gawler's assistant concerning their condition, while the young man, with equal politeness, was endeavouring to exonerate the firm from the charge of being 'beastly damp' (that being the basis of the young woman's argument), but was compelled ultimately to fall back on the saving clause printed on every pawn-ticket, 'that Mr. Gawler was not answerable for moth or rust.'

'How do?' said Uncle Gawler. 'Pretty time to call, of all times in the week, upon my word!' Saying this, he consulted his watch, and, apparently alarmed to find it so late, immediately rushed to the 'spout' and bawled up it, 'Now, you lads! make haste about your tea; there isn't a minute to spare!'

'Why, what may be the matter?' I asked. 'Anything unusual about to happen?'

'Oh no, nothing unusual—the regular thing of Saturday nights,' replied Uncle Gawler, pushing his muscular arms further through his waistcoat-sleeves, as though not at all afraid of the 'regular thing,' but, on the contrary, rather anxious for its approach. 'You won't stay, of course,' continued he; 'they'll be here like a swarm of bees presently, you know, and I shan't have a minute to myself for the next five hours.'

At this moment several of the 'box' doors were heard to open and fall to again with a slam, at which signal Mr. Gawler started and held out his hand to say good-bye. It was evident that those who would presently arrive like a swarm of bees were customers. It was for their reception that my uncle and his assistants had prepared themselves, and taken off their neckcloths and rolled back their sleeves. My resolution was at once taken.

'Shall I be much in your way if I stay for an hour?' I asked.

'My dear fellow!' began Uncle Gawler, while his two young men looked round with astonishment.

'I could sit in the parlour and look through the window,' I suggested. 'I won't disturb you: I'll sit in there as quiet as a mouse.'

'Well, go in if you like,' said Uncle Gawler, after a moment's hesitation; 'you'll soon be glad to get out again, I'll warrant.'

So I went into the little parlour and took a chair at the window in the wall that commanded a fair view of the shop from one end to the other. Especially there was a fair view of the boxes, and, to my surprise, although but five minutes had elapsed since the slamming of the first of the eleven doors had begun, at least forty customers had already assembled. Although, owing to the deep gloom in which the interior of each box was shrouded, it was difficult to make out the figures of the customers, it was easy enough to count their number, for one and all had thrust out a hand containing a small pack of tickets of redemption. It was an odd sight to see this long row of grimy fists and tattered gown and jacket and coat-cuffs all poking towards the shopman and beckoning him coaxingly. However, there was no favouritism. It was quite useless for the owners of the gown-cuffs to address the young man in familiar, not to say affectionate, language, calling him 'David,' and even 'Davy' ('Davy, dear,' one woman called him), or for the jacket-cuffs to growl and adjure David to 'move hisself.' David had a system, and he well knew that the least departure from it would be fatal to the proper conduct of the business of the evening. Beginning at box number one he began the collection of the little squares of pasteboard with both his hands, and 'hand-over-hand,' as one may say, with a dexterity only to be acquired by constant practice, crying out 'tickets! tickets! tickets!' the while. By the time he had perambulated the length of the shop and called at all the boxes he had gathered as many tickets as his fists would hold, and at once turned to a back counter where stood John (the other shopman). John and David then engaged in 'sorting' the tickets, an operation rendered necessary for several reasons. Some of the tickets referred to tools and flat irons and articles of furniture too cumbrous and unwieldy to ascend the 'spout,' and which were accommodated with lodgings in the cellars. Other of the pawn-tickets related to wedding-rings and Sunday brooches and scarf-pins, which were deposited in the room whose walls were mailed with sheet-iron in the rear of the shop. Another reason why the tickets should be sorted was this. A goodly proportion of Uncle Gawler's customers were unacquainted with the art of reading, and not unfrequently tendered tickets pertaining to goods in the custody of another 'uncle' keeping a shop in the neighbourhood, an error if not at once detected likely to lead to a great waste of time and temper.

The tickets sorted, a heavy and melancholy youth, bearing a dark lantern, opportunely emerged from the bowels of the premises through a trap-door in the shop floor, and took into custody the tickets relating to shovels and picks, and saws and planes; while John bustled off with another lantern and the jewellery tickets, and David remained to attend to the 'spout' department. Lapping out at the mouth of the spout, and waving gently to and fro, like the busy tongue of the anteater, was a long leather bag; into this David thrust his handful of cards, and at the same instant briskly touched a bell-handle fixed to the side of the 'spout,' and, with a sudden jerk, the tongue vanished upwards into the maw; to return, however, long and lean as ever, and dangling and wagging as though it had just caught the flavour of the food it was remarkably fond of, and much desired some more.

It must not be supposed that Uncle Gawler himself was meanwhile idle. Redemption was the order of the evening; still, there were numerous cases in which it was necessary rather by way of barter than by ready-money payments. As, for instance, Mrs. Brown, being a laundress, has found it necessary to pawn the table-linen belonging to one of her customers, and, not having money at her command to redeem the same, she feels it convenient to 'put away' the shirts of another customer, and thus make matters square. On Monday she will redeem the shirts of customer number two, by pawning the sheets of customer number three. Or, again, as for instance, the Browns are asked by the Greens to come and have a bit of dinner tomorrow, and have accepted the invitation; but Brown has made a bad week; has not earned enough, indeed, to 'get out' his Sunday coat and the children's frocks. Brown is a man who doesn't like 'to look little.' He won't want his working clothes till Monday; and, as they will be from home, they won't miss the hearthrug. Again, there are exceptions to the rule altogether. Saturday night is a ticklish time for poor mother. No work this week—last week—the week before. Not a single penny. No dinner to-morrow—no dinner on a *Sunday!* Mother does not care. Father does not care—much; but the children! It is all very well to rub along all the week with bread and treacle for the mid-day meal, or, at a pinch, with nothing between breakfast and an 'early tea;' but it is different on Sundays. *Everybody* has dinner on Sunday, even in a Whitecross Street alley; the atmosphere is hazy with the steam of 'bakings;' and by two o'clock you won't find a little pinafore that is not dinner-stained. 'It's of no use,' says poor mother, 'a bit of hot dinner must be got som*how.*' So she waits till dusk, and then, slip-shod in old slippers, carries her sound shoes to Mr. Gawler's and places them on the counter.

This sort of work keeps Uncle Gawler tolerably busy, while his young men are busy restoring the pledged goods; but he is not nearly so busy as he will be presently. By this time the slamming of the box-doors has increased, and a quick succession of dull bumps and thumps announces the descent down the 'spout' of parcels of all sorts and sizes from the various warehouses above. John has returned with the lantern in one hand and a bunch of little packets in the other; and three times the gloomy boy has laboured up the cellar steps, laden with ironware and tools, which he has deposited, with a malicious clatter, upon the shop floor, and once more retreated. The eleven boxes are gradually filling; and from out their gloomy depths, where the clatter and chatter is each moment increasing, there crops a thick cluster of ticket-grasping fists, wriggling to be delivered. But it is not time yet to gather in this second crop: the result of the first, which chokes up the spout, has yet to be cleared off.

This part of the performance is conducted by the indefatigable David. Hauling and tugging at the rag-wrapped bundles that bulge out at the mouth of the spout, he rapidly ranges them, ticket upward (it should have been stated that a duplicate of the ticket held by the pawner is pinned on to the property pawned, and that, when the searchers have found the bundle to which the ticket put into the bag refers, he pins it by the side of the ticket already distinguishing it), and then begins to call out the name the duplicate bears.

'Jones!'

'One; here you are,' somebody calls.

'Three and sevenpence-halfpenny, Jones;' and in a twinkling the money passes one way, and the parcel the other, and Jones is dismissed.

'Robinson! how many, Mrs. Robinson?'

'Five.'

Mrs. Robinson must wait: when the other four bundles happen to turn up, she will get her 'five,' not before; so, putting her first discovered bundle aside, David continues his investigation.

'Mackney! How many, Mackney? Mack-ney!—how many more times am I to holloa?'

'Is it McKenny ye mane?' shouts a shrill voice.

'Well, p'raps it is: what's the article?' inquires the cautious David.

'Siveral,' pipes Mrs. McKenny; 'there's the childers' perrikits, and me ole man's weskit, and a shawl, and——'

'Two and a halfpenny,' exclaims David, cutting the lady cruelly short.

'But I want to part, Davy dear,' said the Irishwoman.

'Why didn't you say so at first?' snapped David, and at the same time tossing the monstrously large two-shilling bundle towards Uncle Gawler.

Uncle Gawler at once seized it, unpinned it, and disclosed petticoats, and shawl, and waistcoat, besides several other articles.

'I want the weskit and shawl, and leave the rist for fifteen pince,' said Mrs. McKenny.

'Ninepence is what you can leave 'em for,' replied Uncle Gawler, with a determination that Mrs. McKenny had not the courage to combat; 'one and four, please.' And having paid this sum, she walked off with the shawl and waistcoat. This at at once explained the meaning of the mysterious placard, 'No parting after eleven o'clock.' It was evident enough that the process of 'parting' was not a little tiresome, and calculated to hamper and impede business if allowed at the busiest time.

The first delivery of pledges over, the second crop of tickets was gathered; and so much heavier was it than the first, that by the time he had reached the sixth box, David's hands were quite full. Big as was the leather bag suspended in the 'spout,' it was chokeful when David thrust in his gathering; and before five minutes had elapsed, the noise of falling bundles within the spout was fast and furious. Tear and haul at them as David might—even with the assistance, slow but determined, of the melancholy cellar-boy—the lads above, now well warmed to their work, were not to be outdone, but kept up the shower, pelt, bump, thump, until the throat as well as the mouth of the spout was fairly choked. Still, in flocked the customers, until there was no more door-slamming, for the boxes were crammed and brimming over into the passage; and the number of ticket-grasping fists that threatened over the counter was enough to appal any but such tried veterans as Uncle Gawler and his crew. Then the uproar! Small-voiced women, of the better sort, begging and entreating of David to take their tickets, at the same time pouring into his adder ears the various domestic businesses on which their need for haste were based. Shrill-voiced women of the worser sort, dirty-faced, baby-bearing, gin-hic-cuppy slatterns, brawling, pushing, driving their elbows into other people's eyes, and trampling on their feet. Drunken men who had never given any ticket at all, and who yet obstinately persisted in blocking up the front and most desirable places, taking great oaths, banging their great fists against the counter, and challenging David into the road to fight. Great indeed must have been the joy of David and John when eleven o'clock struck, and Uncle Gawler shouted 'no more parting!' and, whipping off his sleeved waistcoat, came to their assistance. He was a host in himself. By a few pertinent remarks as to what would be the probable result of their outrageous behaviour when they brought their things back to pledge on Monday morning, he silenced the vixens; and by emphatically declaring that he would not deliver another parcel to his customers until they turned out the noisy drunken men, he got rid of them in a twinkling. He assailed the glutted 'spout,' and delivered bundles in batches of six and eight, and counted up the interest, and took money, and gave change with a celerity that took away one's breath to behold. In half an hour the box doors began again to slam—a sure sign that the rush was thinning: in another twenty minutes he had so slackened the pressure as to find time to come in to me, mopping the perspiration off his scarlet visage with his silk handkerchief, and inquire what I thought of it all.

JAMES GREENWOOD.

TWENTY-FOUR HOURS OF THE SEASON.

BY MY LADY'S WATCH.

OF society's life the first dawning
  Begins with the letters—and yawning !
Your orders you give, while you're sipping
Your tea; then your wrapper on-slipping,

                A.M.
                10.
            She awaketh,

You submit to the toils of the morning—
Your lady's-maid does your adorning;
While you skim, during ornamentation,
The latest three-volume ' sensation.'

    10·30.
   Dresseth,

Next, when you the breakfast-room turn-in,
The children are brought—with the urn—in;
And papa, on the ' Times' intent, drily
Doesn't see that they look at you shily.

    11.
   Breaketh her
   fast.

Babes— and breakfast—disposed of, your jewels
From Hancock's, your dresses from Sewell's,
Your bonnet, your boots, and your chignon
Claim full sixty minutes' dominion.

   Noon—1 p.m.
   Receiveth her
   tradesfolk.

Then off, like a shot from a cannon!—
To horse, and away, the Row's tan on!
Just pausing at times in your canter
Your friends at the railings to banter.

    P.M.
   1—2·30.
   Taketh horse
   exercise.

In your brougham soon shopping you're hieing—
Inspecting—electing—and buying :
Then home, with a cargo of treasures,
For the next in the list of your pleasures.

    3.
   Goeth a-
   shopping.

You then, for a couple of hours, show
Your tasteful toilette at a flow'r show,
Displaying, 'mid roses and orchids,
Light muslins and pale three-and-four kids.

   3—5.
   Visiteth the
   Botanical.

Then, the Royal Academy in, it's
The thing to appear for five minutes.
The merits of Millais and Leighton
It enables you glibly to prate on.

   5—5·10.
   Glanceth at
   the Academy.

But somehow you must be contriving
By six in the Park to be driving.
Your daughter (the eldest, you know,) sits
Beside you—in front of you Flo sits.

    6.
   Taketh car-
   riage exer-
   cise.

Soon homeward you're wearily pressing
With prospects of dinner and dressing.
Faint—aching in every bone—you
Your maid have to eau-de-Cologne you.

   6—6·30.
   Goeth to her
   tiring-room.

Till you meet—the first time since you brake fast—
The being four parsons did make fast
Your slave, at St. George's,—poor sinner !—
And your husband and you have your dinner.

    7—9.
   Hath her
   dinner,

Drawn by Florence Claxto

TWENTY-FOUR HOURS OF THE SEASON
BY MY LADY'S WATCH.

Twenty-four Hours of the Season.

P.M.

9—9·5.
Visiteth her baby.

Fish, soup, entrées, meats, sweets, and cheese are
Brought on—and discussed by degrees are;
Which leaves you five minutes, it may be,
To take just a peep at the baby:—

9·5—9·30.
Goeth to the Opera.

When your maid comes, observing, 'My leddy,
Master says, please, the kerridge is ready;'
And you're off, Covent Garden-wards dashing—
Lamps flashing, wheels splashing and crashing.

9·30—·10.
Enjoyeth music.

And now you display your ecstatic
Devotion for things operatic:—
But the music, you talk so much stuff of,
You find half an hour quite enough of,

11.
Endueth her ball-dress.

Yet a whole one find scarcely suffices
For the various arts and devices,
Which deck you in satin or moiré,
Lace, jewels, and plumes for the soirée,

11 P.M.–12·30.
Showeth her loyalty.

To which you are speedily rushing—
To find there much squeezing and crushing.
The crowd is so great, to get in it's
A matter of quite ninety minutes!

A.M.
1.
Payeth homage to Royalty.

But then, though the struggle dismays you,
The end of it more than repays you!
A smile upon lips that are royal
Rewards your activity loyal.

2—2·30.
Hasteth to a Ball.

You return to your brougham enchanted,
Yet glad of the respite that's granted
For a rest on the carriage's cushion,
To the Countess's Ball while you push on.

3.
Disporteth herself.

But to shake off, soon after arriving,
Your weariness you are contriving,
Coote and Tinney your feet quickly winning
To a waltz-measure, merrily spinning.

4—10.
Retireth to rest.

When at last you get home it just four is!
Every bone of you aching and sore is—
You feel that existence a bore is—
So is going to bed up three stories;—
While the husband you always ignore is
Returned from supporting the Tories
(He M.P. for land-owners galore is),
And, forgetting the House's uproar, is
Asleep—sound as nail in a door is:—
So your greeting just only a snore is;
And you sleep until ten it once more is!

ENGAGED

INTERRUPTED!

'ENGAGED! Oh, indeed! And pray what then, sir?'

'What then, sir? Why, then there is no more insufferable condition for other people than to have to stand by and be spectators of their happiness!'

There is something, after all, in what my friend says, though it can scarcely be supposed he is absolutely serious, considering the advantageous match his daughter, Miss Lucy, has really made of it. That fact being assured, however, he sticks to his point about the discomfort he experiences in being a compulsory witness to 'their extravagant affection.' 'My good friend, you forget. So many things have occupied your attention since the day when you were first admitted to the family circle as the "engaged" of dear Amelia—you seem almost to forget that "dear Amelia" and your excellent wife, "a joyful mother of children," are one and the same person—that you forget both the joy that was yours, and the "insufferable condition" that joy occasioned to the members of your innamorata's family, who received you so kindly. Pray let us hear no more about "extravagant affection." I am as old as you are, and remember well—for was I not, at the very time, in a green and yellow melancholy, sighing for the affections of your dear Amelia's sister Mary, who jilted me in favour of Jack Hornby, the mustachioed and bearded man of war? I remember how eminently ridiculous you were wont to appear to us, who saw not with your eyes, upon almost every occasion when you and dear Amelia figured in public. I will not harrow your feelings by describing what indications of "extravagant affection" you gave when I came unawares, and assuredly without intending it, upon a certain arbour in the garden, where you and yours had sole possession, one Sunday evening in the summer, as I returned from a solitary, unlovely walk. Shall I remind you of the many shifts, more or less flimsy and transparent, with which, many a time and oft, you tried to make your occupation appear other than it had been before you were interrupted by the unwelcome entrance of a third person into the room? Cannot your memory carry you back so far as to the time when you seriously proposed to challenge my cousin Tom, because he, all ignorant of your engagement, dared to take your dear Amelia from under your very eyes, and to waltz with her as he might have done with any young lady whatever? I can remind you, if need be, of the time when you poured out your soul in grief to me, because you were not oftener left alone with your *carissima*, and because her worthy father, a thousand times more amiable than you are, was inconsiderate enough occasionally to require the use of his own study, which, for reasons best known to you and Amelia, was your favourite billing and cooing place.'

Long ago, Charles Lamb raised his voice against the pretensions of the newly married, and held them up to scorn in various ways, in return for indignities which he had suffered at their hands; but the claims and self-assertions of the would-be married have gone on unchecked since long before Lamb's time until now. With the single exception of the bard who Bon Gaultier hight, and who sang in moving verse the miseries of the lover's friend and confidant, no one has ventured to handle the delicate subject of the conduct of engaged people, either towards each other or towards other people. It is a delicate subject, to be sure, and a man might be excused for refraining to bring in the mirth-makers, who haply might select himself for the immediate subject of their laughter. There are so few who can afford to raise a laugh on this subject, so few who have not, once at least in their lives, to pass through the love-making stage, and so to appear, as they say, ridiculous in the eyes of other people. It is a privilege which only old bachelors like myself—I never recovered the blow my young affections received when the beauteous Mary, sister of 'dear Amelia,' threw me overboard for the mustachioed and bearded man of war aforesaid—enjoy. We have a fee simple in the follies and extravagancies both of those who are married, and of those who are about to take upon them the holy estate of matrimony; we can with impunity let 'our jest among our friends be free,' and in the matter of courtship—as they used to call it in my young days—we have a right to comment upon it as we like, because of the completeness with which we are excluded from the joys of it. I hold that my friend, who grumbles at the 'insufferable condition' in which he is placed, is quite out of court. He does but see the reflection of his former self; it is an instance of the thing that hath been being the same that shall be; and, so far as he is concerned by it, there is no new thing under the sun. With me it is different. Though once in my life, as I have already hinted, I 'sat like patience on a monument,' smiling at the grief which the mustachioed and bearded man of war caused me in the matter of Mary, sister to 'dear Amelia,' I sighed to myself only, without declaring my passion, and had not, therefore, to go through any public exhibitions of 'extravagant affection,' such as, doubtless, I should have done had I been admitted to *pratique*, and had the Fates been kinder to me than they were. Thus, you see, gentle readers, I am at liberty to make any remarks I please upon the situation. No one can meet me with a *tu quoque*, or declare me estopped from using as freely as I like the gleanings of my experience. Let my friend therefore, for decency's sake, stand aside, and let me take his place. I am vain enough to think I shall treat the matter with a hand more tender and more sympathetic than his, while I shall not the less expose what he would in his unamiability tear to tatters.

There is, then, to be noticed in the carriage and deportment of engaged persons an amount of awkwardness and restraint in the presence of other people, which not only stamp them for what they are, but tend to make the whole party amongst whom they find themselves perfectly uncomfortable. Strangers —that is to say, any people but the two who are interested in maintaining the monopoly of mutual 'extravagant affection'—feel almost guilty at being the occasion of so much discomfort. They do not want to obtrude themselves on the attention of the loving pair; and assuredly, if their own personal comfort were alone concerned, they would get far out of sight of the enamoured; but circumstances will not admit of it; there must be certain rooms in common at certain times—under no circumstances, for instance, do lovers, love they never so lovingly, quite dispense with the service of the dining-room. Common civility, moreover, requires that occasionally they should be in the drawing-room, or other place where the other members of the family are assembled; and it is on each and all of these occasions that the characteristics above mentioned are noticeable. There is in the manner and on the face of Amandus an expression half of listlessness, half of anxiety to be agreeable in spite of himself, which strikes a disinterested observer rather curiously. He begins to think that Amandus is unwell, that he is a genius pondering abstruse questions 'even in the presence;' or may be the thought crosses his brain, as he sees the continuousness of Amandus's absence of mind, that perchance he may have committed some crime which makes him ill at ease. Only one who is cognizant of the true state of the case can rightly interpret the meaning of that shifting glance of the eyes, that perpetual wandering to and fro the beloved object, who sits uncomfortably upon some neighbouring chair or sofa, and tries to play the hypocrite, though with as poor a result as Amandus. As plainly as the expression on an intelligent being's countenance can convey a meaning, so plainly is it apparent to the disinterested unappropriated that Amandus is chafing on the bit which good manners have forced into his mouth, and that he is wishing with all his heart he had wings like a bird, that he might fly into the study or the breakfast-room, where he would be with Amanda. What pleasure, what satisfaction there can be in thus secluding himself with Amanda I do not pretend to say. Would it not seem more glorious to stay in the midst of the family circle, and triumph openly and continuously in the conquest you have won? Or are there sweet mysteries, solemn rites of courtship, which none but the initiated may know, and which must be performed in so private a manner, that the sudden entry of a Philistine into the room is enough to scare the votaries of Cupid from their vow-making, and to cause a trepidation that is observable long after the invader has entered? I presume it must be so, else there could not be so great, so manifest a desire on the part of Amandus and Amanda, and on the part of Amanda's father before them, as I have already testified, to get away to some covert from the common gaze.

'*Not* that room! *They* are in there!'

'Confound them! Suppose they are? My "Encyclopædia Britannica" is in there too; and surely I may go and fetch it!'

'My dear sir, you are too violent, and too inconsiderate as well. At all events, make a noise with the door-handle, so as to give some warning of your coming.'

My friend feels the awkwardness of having his own study as effectually sealed against him as if the Customs officers had found out that he had an illicit distillery in it: he resents what he calls an encroachment on his liberty; but the noise he has made in stumbling over the door-mat, and in fumbling with the door-handle, has put 'the pair' sufficiently on the *qui vive* to allow of their quitting the celebration of those rites unknown to all but the initiated, and my friend enters his study to find his large easy chair vacant, but looking as if it had not long been so, drawn up in a comfortable position on one side of the fireplace, while Amandus, who might be suspected of having sat therein, is busy seeing 'why the lamp burns so dimly,' and Amanda, at the other end of the room, is so ostentatiously engaged in looking over some music, that one is bound to suppose with Longfellow that 'things are not what they seem.' It does not require one thoroughly acquainted with the rites of Dan Cupid to conjecture that Amandus and Amanda had been differently occupied ere that fumbling with the door-handle warned them of the fact that a Philistine was approaching.

'Two are company, three none,' says Marian, when it is proposed that she shall go with Amandus and Amanda to the croquet party at Mrs. Thingumby's. 'You are quite right, my dear;' only there is the slightest possible tinge of dissatisfaction in your tone that you are of the three, and not of the two, which leads one to doubt whether your remark is prompted so much by a desire to let the company consist of the only harmonious elements, as by a wish to point uncomfortably towards the composition of the company in order to gratify yourself by enjoying their discomfort. If the tone be rightly interpreted, I will pass by your remark as being merely cynical; if not, I humbly beg your pardon, and cordially endorse the truism you have uttered. Engaged folk *do*, as a matter of fact, dislike the presence of a third person, almost as much, perhaps more, than that of a large party. 'A great company is a great solitude,' and in it the 'engaged' can be, comparatively speaking, free, almost unnoticed; whereas, in narrower limits they both cause and are required to give a greater attention. I am far from being certain that the condition of the third person who is tacked on to the 'happy pair' is not much more 'insufferable' than theirs. If they so far consider him or her as not to talk about themselves, it will be in so forced and artificial a manner as to make their conversation less tolerable than their silence, or their mutual self-appropriation. With what unblushing selfishness do an engaged couple walk off together, with a *noli nos tangere* expression on their faces, as though they had a monopoly of the earth on which they walk, and would resent any intrusion as the infringement of a patent right. Whilst they choose to walk they are as scarecrows to the timid and the good natured, who avoid them as tabooed objects, and 'steal away so guilty like,' if perchance they stumble upon them in the course of their perigrinations. My friend, the father of Amanda, speaks very feelingly on this subject. He says his favourite part of the garden is no longer one of his pleasant places; the ivy-grown summer-house, where he was wont to read and smoke a lazy pipe, is no longer available for him since he was foolishly led to sanction the mad engagement which brings his Amanda and her Amandus so much in his way.

He complains, too—and herein, as a calm, dispassionate observer, I am compelled to join with him—of the demonstrativeness of the 'engaged.' 'Positively, sir, I have seen them sitting knee to knee almost, with their hands clasped, their tongues as silent as the grave, their eyes reflecting all sorts of nonsense from one to the other, and looking like the most perfect fools that can be met with out of Bedlam.'

Gently, my friend. This fault, this unshamefaced glorying, if you will, is very reprehensible. If it does nothing else it asserts to all present, more plainly than is agreeable, that they are not happy as the engaged are; but there is no need for you to break out into a fury on the subject. I will mention the circumstance in a don't-do-it-again sort of way through the various circles of London Society, and I doubt not you will cease to be troubled by demonstrations of 'extravagant affection.'

Did the captain take Amanda down to dinner? Well, it was very *gauche* in the hostess not to have arranged differently; but there is no reason why you, Amandus, should sit savagely all dinner-time, saying nothing whatever to the amiable lady by your side, who is ignorant of your misfortune, and is trying to enlist your sympathies in the last report of the Society for procuring a change in the colour of the Ethiopian's skin. Do not venture to press Amanda's foot, though you may think it to be within reach, under the table. You can assure her of your sentiments towards her as well as of those you entertain towards the captain afterwards. Meantime, though you may think to touch Amanda's foot with your own, it may happen you light accidentally on the captain's, and some embarrassment may ensue.

Why should you be angry because an old friend of Amanda's chooses to talk to her longer than you like? Is it not enough for you that Amanda has preferred you to the old friend, to all her old friends, and only wishes not to make *them* feel the preference too keenly? Go to; you are unreasonable!

Again, while I recommend you not to wear your heart on your sleeve for daws to peck at, or, in other words, not to flaunt your engagement in everybody's face, be particularly careful how you inflict upon your friends the story 'How you did thrive in this fair lady's love, and she in yours.' Your lady friends will perhaps welcome the recital, for their tender, loving natures incline them to listen to a tale of love; but your male friends, glad enough to know that you are happy, will vote you a bore if you give them too many details of your happiness. They will be sure to discount your description of your ladylove; it is ten to one they will make fun of you and of her too, the ungenerous brutes, in the next conversation they have with a mutual friend; they will think but simply of you for talking of that which you should keep as private as possible; and they will wish you at Jericho if you take up much of their time with a matter in which they can have but a specially limited interest.

'It is the most egregious bore
Of all the bores I know,
To have a friend who lost his heart
A short time ago.'

This will be the burden of their song, this will be the true expression of their inmost feelings; and though good-nature may prompt them to bear and forbear, they will assuredly feel aggrieved if you draw, as the custom of lovers is, upon their patience *ad libitum*.

As for Amanda, it would be almost presumptuous in me to offer her any counsel, yet, at the risk of offending so charming a young lady, I will venture to suggest that she should be very chary of confiding too much to her 'dearest Jane' or Lucy. The chances are she will say more than she intended, and there will be some additions made by lively imaginations. Let her remember she has some one else's confidence to keep besides her own. Let not the love of triumph, the communicative springs of happiness, still less the mere love of 'hearing or telling some new thing,' lead her into imparting thoughts which are already 'engaged.' Let her not exult by word or action, as I have seen some do, over her compeers who are unattached; 'there is many a slip,' &c. Above all, let her consider very tenderly the abnormal position in which she and all about her are placed during the term of her engagement—let not that be long—and let her try to accommodate herself to the convenience—ay, even to the prejudices of those whom she is soon to leave, and to whom she will thereafter be glad that she showed so much consideration and self-denial. Finally, let her not on any account forget to ask me to the wedding. She may rely upon my services in the matter of giving away, of speech-making, of flinging the slipper, of drying the tears of the respective mothers-in-law, of anything, in short, which may properly and fairly be considered as forming part of the office and duty of the devoted admirer of all Amandas.

F. W. R.

HUMOURS OF THE PARIS EXHIBITION.

ENOUGH has been said about the Paris Exhibition in the way of description and criticism, and, to state a candid impression candidly, I think it has been overpraised and overwritten about. But before it closes' let me gather up some personal reminiscences and a few additions of adventure that will keep clear of the newspapers. Going about among one's friends and acquaintances, Paris has been the prominent idea all the spring and summer. When I lunched lately with the Griggses of Clapham Park (old Griggs being safely stowed away at the Stock Exchange), mamma and the girls told me that though they had certainly been bitten by Overend and Gurney, they had made up their minds (old Griggs having always kept within a margin) that it was absolutely necessary, particularly with respect to public opinion in Clapham Park, that they should do the Exhibition. How excited the dear girls became when they talked about the amusements and dissipations of Paris, for which the Exhibition would furnish colour and excuse; and how unreservedly did Mrs. Griggs take me into confidence about Overend and Gurney; and how glad she was to find that she was not absolutely obliged to go to the Grand Hôtel or the Louvre, and that every meal would not necessarily cost a napoleon a head. Griggs asked me a few days after to partake of a saddle of mutton, which meant a gorgeous dinner, in which there was no apparent falling off from pristine splendour. At the dinner I certainly contrasted the lofty politeness of the young ladies with the cozy familiarity of the lunch, and I am afraid I thought worthy Mrs. Griggs a humbug for alluding in that distant way to the Paris Exhibition, as if it were a subject that had only lately and accidentally entered her thoughts. I knew that Griggs would have to submit; it was only a matter of time; and sure enough the Griggses turned up, as will be hereafter mentioned in this veracious narrative. Likewise several friends of mine rushing into matrimony about this time, despite my gentle dissuasives, which met with less attention than my valuable remarks ordinarily received, I was much consulted on the advisability of proceeding to Paris for the honeymoon. I quite admitted that in one point of view there was a great deal to be said for the idea. You will not be bored with each other so soon, having the Exhibition to fall back upon. Poor Widdicombe, who was married the other day, about a week after the event, had to telegraph to some friends to join him, as he and his bride were tired of each other's society. Still, in crossing the Channel, you may be placing yourself and your wife under very unromantic conditions. Supposing one or both of you are very ill, you will either be making yourself ridiculous at the very time when you would wish to be most interesting, or beginning to signalise yourself too early for brutal indifference. However, several braces of married pairs disregarded my advice, and on some far-distant day they will probably acknowledge to me that they regretted they did not follow it. Then, again, there were a whole lot of undergraduates from Trinity, who went over *en masse*, and did not even think it necessary to make any pretence of a coach and private readings. I was hardly surprised to find my own old college friend, Jones, at the Exhibition, for wherever I go I meet Jones as a matter of course. He is a special correspondent to some paper, and at the present moment is getting his traps together to be off to Abyssinia. But I confess I was very much and agreeably surprised to see my friend the Rev. Theophilus Gataker, who for the last thirty-five years has been immured in a rectory in Dorsetshire, during which time he has hardly visited London, turning up on the Boulevards, and placidly imbibing sherry cobbler at an American bar. But we live in an era of revolutions, and Mr. Gataker's revolutionary movements struck me more forcibly as a sign of the times than Mr. Disraeli's Household Parliament.

As I was staying for a little while at Calais, it was a great amusement to check off the different people who were passing to and fro. About this time the balance of summer weather had been seriously disturbed. Violent winds had set in, and on the narrow seas it alternately blew a quarter, a half, and a whole gale. Travellers tell us of a certain halfway station, I think somewhere on the Andes, where a singular contrast is presented between the ascending and descending travellers who meet at the same point. Those who are mounting are shivering with cold, and those who are descending are fainting with heat. Not otherwise was the scene at Calais. Jaunty, well-dressed, and smiling were the travellers who had just come back from Paris; miserable, disorderly, and in the deepest dejection were those who had just landed from Dover. These looked cheerily at the sky and took weather observations on the quay, as if they could thus obtain the smallest indication of the state of matters in the middle of the Channel; those were thoroughly beaten, and, asking for bedrooms and brandy, declared their utter inability to proceed to Paris on the same day. Jones alone was unmoved. He told me that he had been twice round Cape Horn, and had spent a considerable part of his life upon the Bay of Biscay. As for one of the lovely young brides who showed up on this occasion, I am afraid that even thus early in the gushing spring of life she had arrived at the conclusion, speaking metaphorically, that matrimony is not all beer and skittles. She had considerably picked up next morning, and by extraordinary efforts at matronly demeanour, endeavoured to convince the breakfast-table world that she was celebrating her silver or twenty-fifth wedding-day, instead of being fresh from St. George's, Hanover Square. But even more than those who had suffered in their passage I pitied those who were about to make it—

'Unheeding of the sweeping whirlwind's sway,
Which, hush'd in grim repose, awaits its evening prey.'

I had been in the Avenue Labourdonnaye, looking at the Belgian collection of pictures, when I saw the Griggses approach the office for issuing weekly tickets. The elderly Griggs had been profoundly penetrated with the idea, while on the Stock Exchange one day, that the proper thing was to take the weekly ticket, whereby an entire admission was secured, also a free pass to all the *péages spéciaux*, and you might go in and out as often as you liked and at any entrance. This is all very true, and the Griggses were in the right to take weekly tickets; only they ought to have remembered, for I had given them the hint, that they must be provided with photographs, to which their weekly ticket is added. But somehow they had imbibed the imbecile idea that in the case of Britishers this rule was not very strictly insisted on, little knowing the Gallic passion for organization and the Median strictness of their regulations. They had all the consolations which shrugs and smiles could impart, but the rules were inexorable; and all the officials could do was to point out to them a photographic establishment where their *cartes de visite* might be taken with the least possible delay. So Mr. and Mrs. Griggs, and Master Griggs, and the two Miss Griggses had to dangle about a photographic studio for the whole of the morning, and the old birds did not at all appreciate the fifty francs which formed the initial expense of the Exhibition. They would have saved time and money if they had had minds open to conviction. Laura Griggs is a very nice girl, that is to say, as nice as any girl of the name of Griggs can be, and the sooner she changes it the better. I have my doubts, however, whether she would consider the name of Tompkins any improvement; I am afraid that Griggs *père* would consider it an impecunious name. Chatting with Laura in the studio was very pleasant for a time, but I question if even Petrarch himself could have stood very much of Laura, if a grilling sun was glowering through a glass roof, and the dust was an inch deep on the bare floors and the mutilated chairs, and grinning idiots came and went on the same monotonous errand connected with their inexpressive countenances, and a very strong smell of chemicals was pervading the establishment, and the British father was loudly excerating the stupidity of his wife in not bringing the photographs and the stupidity of the French in wanting them, and there were seventeen flights of stairs to traverse between the *atelier* and the *entresol*. It was edifying to meet Mr. Griggs some hours later, with a little library packed under his arm, containing an entire and unique collection of the catalogues, and addressing himself to the systematic study of the different objects. I made the mental calculation that this enthusiasm for knowledge would continue till Griggs should arrive at the British refreshment department, when Griggs would assuredly subside into a state of bottled stout. There was one particular scientific object which received considerable attention from my friend. This consisted of the plans and sections of a contemplated railway across the Channel. I wonder if the ingenious framer of those plans ever had any actual experience of a gale in a Channel. The notion of any bridge of boats ever spanning the waves under a sou' wester is one of the most marvellous and incongruous that could ever have occurred to the imagination of an architect of Laputa. When we had cleared out of Dover we had found ourselves at once in the teeth of a gale, and a sea behind (the *undæ sequaces* of Horace) swept clean over the deck, and Laura Griggs had been enveloped at once in a sheet of water, and might have imagined herself in bathing costume beneath the briny. I need hardly say that there was a manly form at hand on whose stalwart arm she could find support. After the bottled stout Mr. Griggs was not long in steering his way to one of those deep leather-covered circular settees which are infinitely more comfortable than any of the chairs, for which two sous are demanded. Here the worthy man reclined, and spread a yellow silk pocket-handkerchief over his head and deliberately composed himself to sleep. Quite a circle of admiring Frenchmen gathered round him, and I confidently expect to find him reproduced in the 'Charivari' shortly. In the meanwhile I pioneered the ladies to the *Jardin réservé*, and envied the cool fishes that were swimming about so leisurely in their aquarium. In that cool grot Laura was accidentally separated from her party, but I had impressed upon them the precaution that in case of any such accident they should resort to the pavilion of coinage in the central garden at the stroke of the hour. Dazed and amazed to the last degree were the Griggses on their first day, and I quite pitied Laura, who would have revivified if the poor girl could have had a quarter of an hour's rest from the incessant tumult and noise.

One day I had mentioned this fact to Jones, how this restless Exhibition tired one so soon, and that I should enjoy it doubly if only I could get a little repose and read my morning 'Galignani,' which has the same sedative effect for me as a morning pipe. 'Come along with me,' said Jones, tapping me upon the shoulder. Then Jones led me into a large cool room, spacious and silent, where a large table was literally covered with newspapers and periodicals, and little tables had writing materials and blotting-papers; and better than all was the enjoyment of ease and privacy, and the consciousness that out of that surging human sea I had planted my foot on dry land at last. 'Oh, Jones, this *is* kind!' I said, as I wrung his hand and a manly tear started to my eye. 'What jolly club is this? Put me down as a visitor, or make me a member. Expense is no object.' Then Jones grimly smiled, and pointed me to the printed bill, 'Working Man's Hall.' 'Jones,' I said, 'I will be a working man. Ease before dignity. I will wear corduroys and a blouse before I lose this paradise of the Exhibition.' I may here mention, parenthetically, that very few corduroys and blouses ever came into this fairy hall, which was a secluded deserted island in the middle of the waste. 'Tompkins,' said Jones, 'if you were the British aristocrat, or a bloated capitalist, or a man of letters and genius, you might sigh in vain for admission into this palatial hall. Labour is king. The British workman is the ruling influence of the state, and you may judge of his supremacy by the fact that the only place at all approximating to a club in the Exhibition has been appropriated to the British workman, and the man of mere education and refinement has no retreat of the kind.' Jones is a fellow of infinite resource. He contrived, greatly to my delight, to present me with a ticket of membership, and I was quite prepared to coalesce with the British working man, who so rarely turned up, however, that I had no opportunity of extending to him the grasp of brotherhood. Jones knows a lot of queer things. I cannot think how he manages to pick up his information, only I know that he, or rather the people who own him, will give any amount of money to get it. He has repeatedly told me important items of Paris news the evening before they appeared in the Paris morning papers. 'There was a queer story going a little while ago,' said Jones, 'at the time the Emperor distributed the prizes at the Palais in the Champs Elysées. You were there, I suppose?' said Jones. I was compelled to own that I was not. 'I was, though, and not so very far from the imperial dais. The story is,' he continued, lowering his voice, 'that when some man belonging to the electric telegraph came to receive his prize from the hands of the Emperor, he slipped into his hands a paper, on which he had written, *Maximilian is taken, and shot.* It was the first intelligence that had come to Europe, and amid all the splendours of the scene, the Emperor quailed visibly. Curious story, isn't it, Tompkins?' said Jones. 'Do you believe it?' I inquired. Jones was silent, and declined to answer. 'I didn't put it into the paper,' he added, 'but, for all that, so ran the story at the time, and I observed that it got into one of the foreign newspapers.'

Those Griggses were certainly the most helpless people in the world, thoroughly unversed in Parisian ways, and with all my regard for Laura's belongings, the thing became rather 'a grind.' It was quite a separate piece of education to teach them how to get to the Exhibition. I used to convey them safely to the railway station in the Rue d'Amsterdam, where they could not go far wrong, as the line set them down within the very building itself. Then, for a change, I took them through the Louvre to the steamers, where, on the river, they always found a fresh breeze, and, boating between the quays, saw the finest view which Paris could offer. It was I who showed them that they need not necessarily be cheated by the coach-drivers, and explained to them the mystery of the correspondence of omnibuses. It was I who enabled them to navigate their own course in triumph to the Porte Rapp. It was I who was their escort to St. Germains, St. Cloud, and Fontainebleau, and, instead of allowing them to tread in the beaten track of tourists, took them to choice bits of genuine forest scenery in these regions, which, by themselves, they could never have found out. But why should I enumerate all the boons I showered upon this family, whose ingratitude —but I must not anticipate the tragic portion of my narrative. The Griggses had gone to an hotel in one of the streets between the Champs Elysées and the Faubourg St. Honoré, the heart of the English quarter. They had got a floor to themselves, almost as complete as a Scotch flat, and Mrs Griggs, having the recollection of Overend and Gurney before her, had resolved to make the matutinal coffee herself, and not have it sent up from the hotel. I met Griggs rushing about the Faubourg one morning, and he asked me, in a distracted state of mind, what was the French for coffee-pot. I helped him out of his difficulty, and saw him return to his inn with the humble but comforting article surreptitiously concealed beneath his overcoat. The dining difficulties that beset the Griggses were very great. They had gone into a café and demanded dinner, but Laura, whose boarding-school French had been confidently relied on, broke down altogether under the test, and Mr. and Mrs. Griggs, finding that they could make nothing of the carte that had been handed to them, majestically sailed out into the streets. I gave them a good dinner and a pleasant evening on one occasion, but I could not always be doing that sort of thing. We dined together at the Cercle International — about ten francs a head, including wine - after we had had a long afternoon at pictures, and then sat out in the open air, listening to the music of Strauss' band; then we drove to the hotel for coffee, and afterwards went to the Théâtre Lyrique, where, with incredible pains, I had managed to secure a box for the performance of Romeo et Juliette. That was really a great thing for Laura Griggs, for it enabled her to compare among her friends Patti's personation of Juliette with that of Madame Miolan-Carvalho, for whom Gounod composed the music. In fairness perhaps, it ought to be mentioned that old Griggs performed the useful but subordinate part of paymaster. I myself lean to the opinion that the charges against the French for imposition are, upon the whole, rather exaggerated, and that they are no worse than the Londoners were in 1862. Yet I must allow that the Griggses were grossly victimized in the matter of their dinners at the hotel. There was certainly an announcement in thin gold letters that there was a table-d'hôte à 6 heures. I flatter myself that I know something of the tables-d'hôte of Paris, and I venture to say that for years there had been no regular table-d'hôte at that hotel. The salle-à-manger totally contradicted all the received notions about French cleanliness and glitter, being dark and bare and repellent. The Griggses were surprised that they were always dining alone, and that the dinners contradicted all their notions respecting the glories of French cookery. I dined with them one day in a friendly way—what old Gilbert called ' promiscuous-like '— and took mental as well as bodily stock of the feed—a very thin soup, no fish, bif-stack (sic), and pommes-de-terre, haricot verts, gigot de mouton, volaille (microscopic merry-thoughts), and lettuces drenched in oil. Voilà tout! The dessert was not bad, and old Gilbert gave us champagne ad libitum. He complained to me bitterly of his French dinners. 'They are not so bad,' I replied, ' provided you take a sufficient number of them in the course of the day.' I had no doubt but the landlord procured the dinners from a neighbouring restaurant, and charged napoleons where he had paid francs. Griggs showed me his bill for the week, which, when stated in francs, sounded enormous. I explained to him that for much less he might dine very well at the Palais Royal or on the Boulevards, and for not much more he might dine sumptuously at Dotesio's or Philippe's. The old gentleman explained that they were most days at the Exhibition, and always had a solid lunch at Spiers and Pond's, or

Bertram and Roberts's. I invited them to come and dine with me on the Boulevards, and I was this time the real host. It was an immense room, and the ladies looked almost frightened. There was certainly the drawback of some questionable people present, and I was afraid that I had got myself into a scrape, but my worthy friends were none the wiser. They enjoyed taking their coffee on the Boulevards, although rather nervous that their presence there might not be quite *comme il faut*, but safe under their double guardianship.

James, of Trinity, was perhaps the most interesting member of the group of Cantabs. Just before he came abroad he had received a legacy of two thousand pounds, and I think the receipt of this legacy had something to do with his coming abroad, for, as they say of children, the money was burning a hole in his pocket. He said that the interest would not be of the slightest use to him, and that therefore it would be advisable to expend the principal. After all, he was not so very extravagant, and the men around him were not men who would allow him to be extravagant on their account. But we saw no objection to his giving us a little dinner, to celebrate the virtues of the deceased relative who had left him this unexpected windfall. It was certainly the best dinner which I had during my last trip to Paris. It was at the Trois Frères. I will just mention some details, as it will be interesting to some persons to know how people *can* dine in Paris. The arrangement for the dinner was thirty francs a head, exclusive of wines. Of wines there was every conceivable kind, and of the best; no bottle cost less than a napoleon, and no glass of *liqueur* less than three francs. The dishes were sent up in endless multiplicity, and, of course, an immense number of them were necessarily sent away untasted. The waiters had a sovereign between them. The expense of the dinner to its hospitable donor was a little over five pounds a head.

The next day I had been endeavouring to improve my mind in the useful and industrial part of the Exhibition. I had wandered over the trackless wastes devoted to dry manufactured goods, a display in which the French certainly beat us from the simple circumstance that the English manufacturers with remarkable unanimity abstained from exhibiting. Still fired by the same noble thirst for knowledge, I examined many models of engines, but when I attempted to take some sketches I was speedily brought to an anchor by the prohibitions of the police. Then I listened to the multitudinous clanging of the clocks proclaiming the hour, and thinking of Charles the Fifth and his difficulty at Yuste in making his clocks keep time, a secret which the French clockmakers have not altogether succeeded in solving. Suddenly I heard a great cheering and shouting, and from corridors and picture galleries the people came rushing forth in that excitement which so rapidly flares up in a large concourse, and outside there was cheering, laughing, and gesticulations. Could it be the Emperor? I thought. Could Queen Victoria suddenly have changed her mind and come over? A moment's reflection told me that emperors and queens could hardly have caused all that excitement. At one time they were to be seen almost any day at the Exhibition, noiselessly pursuing their work of examination in an orderly, business-like way, glad to escape any attention; and if a mob of gazers gathered around, a cordon was quickly formed, the approaches intercepted, and the royal view confined to those who first caught sight of it. Dashing forth to inquire what it was that had disturbed the French people from their conventional propriety, my wandering gaze encountered the following spectacle. On a moveable fauteuil sat James of Trinity, triumphantly waving his hat and insisting on favouring the mob with a specimen of British eloquence. A procession of nine other fauteuils followed in order, consisting of James' set, and various other young men whom they had met accidentally at one of the restaurants, and with whom they had gloriously amalgamated. Then after lunch the idea of the procession occurred to them. I was astonished to recognise the intellectual features of Jones among the Corybantic inhabitants of the fauteuils. They explained afterwards that there had been no regular procession since the opening of the building, and something of the kind was sadly wanted. The astonishment of the onlookers was great when they saw the chairs usually appropriated to invalids or weaklings filled with a set of stalwart young men, under the influence of a lunch rather too much on the scale of the dinner of the preceding day. I lost sight of the procession as it rapidly proceeded to round the circle. The magic word 'Anglaises' whispered and rapidly caught up among the crowd seemed fully to account for any eccentricity or lunacy which the young men had displayed.

A friend of Mr. James, whom we will call Rolle, had chosen to fall in love with one of the young women who belonged to one of the restaurants. It was not the young maid at the Tunisian café, who monotonously sings all day long 'Oh we shall all be glad when Johnny comes marching home,' which her cosmopolitan audience is convinced is one of the vernacular melodies of North Africa. Neither was it a French vivandière with her heroic associations, nor yet one of those Tyrolese or Bavarian peasants who in the picturesque costume of their country hand you the wholesome goblet of foaming beer. It was, I believe, some English maiden, and Rolle fell a victim to a fine head of hair. At the Exhibition, English beauty, at least at the restaurants, chiefly runs into hair. 'Hair is a difficult and curious subject, Mr. Rolle,' said Jones, giving me a sly nod, as we three sat one night at M. Draher's, making an impartial and scientific comparison between the beer of Vienna and our country's 'bitter.' 'Are you aware, Mr. Rolle, that the subject of the human hair has greatly occupied the attention of the commissioners, and as the chignon has convincingly shown how comparatively scanty is the natural supply, the promotion of the natural growth has become a serious object of public interest. It would hardly do to make such a matter the subject of public competition, but I believe I am correct in stating that an intimation was given to respective restaurateurs that quantity of hair was requisite for those who should assist behind the counters, and substantial prizes would be privately conferred. I believe, Mr. Rolle, that the young lady who spends so much of her time in compounding iced drinks for you has obtained either a silver medal or honourable mention.' I do not know whether Rolle altogether appreciated Jones's irony, for he was 'true Yorkshire bred— strong in the back and weak in the head.' It is of Rolle's strength of back and weakness of head that I am about to speak. We need not go further into the history of his admiration for that head of hair. The owner thereof used regularly to administer sherry cobbler and brandy-smash to Mr. Rolle by the hour; but if he became at all amatory in his attentions he was promptly consigned to the attendance of a grinning waiter. As a matter of fact, after Rolle had probably injured his constitution by the number and variety of his iced and aërated drinks (not to speak of the corresponding detriment to his substance) he withdrew in disgust as other men had done both before and after him. At the present time, however, it was the custom of Mr. Rolle to spend the concluding hours of the evening at this restaurant, when he found the coast tolerably clear and he might more leisurely pursue his little game. For myself, I found that the evening hours at the Exhibition were intolerably dull. A spasmodic effort had been made to represent them as peculiarly brilliant, and to persuade the public that the hours between the closing of the building and the closing of the park were of the most cheerful and festive kind. But the show was closed and the lights none, and the crowds thin and thinner except in the immediate neighbourhood of the restaurants, and the attempts to impart to the Exhibition nights an Arabian character utterly collapsed. As having a special object at this time, Mr. Rolle never failed to present himself towards the conclusion of each day's proceedings. One evening, however, he was later than the half-hour beyond which there was no admission. He endeavoured to argue the case with the officials in husky English and still more indifferent French. The French logic, that of keeping the rules, is always of a remorseless character. Then Rolle retired within himself, steps a few steps back, collects all the strength in his back, and at a bound cleared the barrier. Immediately the gens d'armes seized him—and he ought to have had the sense to know that any resistance would have been utterly futile and foolish. Then Rolle struck out right and left, and materially marred the Gallic visage before he was overpowered by superiority of weight. At the moment when Jones and I caught sight of him two of the French police had their fists in his neck-tie and Rolle was showing every sign of approximate suffocation. At our urgent entreaty the detaining grasp was withdrawn, and then Rolle struck wildly out and perpetrated a series of assaults for which a Bow Street magistrate would have sent him to prison without the alternative of a fine. He was immediately led off to some cells, and Jones, who understands all sorts of things, told me that Rolle could not possibly get off under a fortnight's imprisonment. We followed the police to see what we could do; and I will do Jones the justice of saying that he came out nobly, and spoke most eloquently in excuse of Rolle. I perceived with astonishment that the police evidently knew Jones, and very favourably, but Jones knows everybody. To my great joy Rolle was discharged; but as soon as the infatuated idiot was told of this he used violent language to all the Frenchmen present and wanted to fight them all round. The result of this was that he was remanded to a cool cell for a couple of hours, and then unconditionally released: the French authorities acting throughout with extraordinary leniency and good temper, and excusing a great deal on the ground of insular lunacy.

I am glad to think that I was able to be of some service to Mr. Gataker. That worthy divine was thoroughly unsettled in mind and body by his separation from all those English habits amid which he had attained an old age. But I showed him that an England existed even in Paris, and that by a slight effort of fancy he might not be much worse off than in London. I took him to Galignani's reading-room in the Rue de Rivoli, where he was almost as comfortable as at his club, and to English eating-houses, where he would hear much more English than French, and have English chops and English steaks and not the French counterfeits; and having a taste for English theatricals (for he belonged to the old school who had no objection to a play once in a way) I took him to the Italiens, where Mr. Sothern was performing Lord Dundreary to the delight of the English and the puzzledom of the French. At this time Lord Dundreary's intelligent countenance was *affiché* all over Paris to an extent to which the human countenance had never been *affiché* before. The acting, as usual, was of consummate excellence, but the audiences were deplorably thin; most of the resident English and American families had left Paris for the summer. Mr. Gataker wandered about recklessly through the never-ending galleries, but he was in a new world, and he told me that in his seventieth year he did not now care to talk its dialect and pick up its knowledge. He would slip away from the Exhibition in the afternoon, and his tall, venerable, slightly bent figure might be discerned in the direction of the Anglo-American Episcopal Church for the afternoon service. Yet there was much instruction and wisdom to be derived from the simple remarks of my old friend, albeit he acknowledged he was as much at a loss on the plain of Mars as he should have been on the plain of Shinar. One afternoon he went with me through the department of arms and ammunition. The good old man looked rather sad. Even to his uncritical eye the matchless art and perfection of our armoury was visible; and certainly no other country has sent out a warlike display equal to that issued from Woolwich. 'It is very silly of us,' said the old-fashioned rector, 'to allow the secrets of our strength to be thus exposed. It is just like Hezekiah showing his treasures to the Assyrians, and we may yet have bitterly to rue our folly. I had a brother once, sir, an elder brother, who was killed in the retreat from Affghanistan, poor fellow! and when I was a lad he took me over Woolwich Arsenal, and though I knew nothing about these matters, I am able just to discern that there have been wonderful improvements. Otherwise it is all Greek to me; or rather,' added the old man, as the recollection of ancient academic triumphs glittered in his eye, 'I could manage Greek, but I could not manage the subject of artillery. I only wish that the art of peace had made the same progress as the art of war.' I repeated the lines—

'Ah! when shall all men's good
Be each man's aim, and universal peace
Lie like a line of light across the land,
And like a lane of beams athwart the sea,
Through all the compass of the golden year?'

He nodded approvingly. 'Mr. Tennyson, my dear sir, did you say? It is very pretty indeed. A .very rising young man, I believe; only I wish he would turn his abilities to something else than poetry. When we have got all the great old poets, Dryden, and Pope, and Milton, and Gray, and Goldsmith, I do not see what need we have got of any more poetry, at all events until people know the old ones thoroughly first, which is certainly not the case in my part of the world. But we are only slow swifts, as the saying is, down in Berkshire.' When I pointed out to him the ambulances and medicine-chests for the wounded, and reminded him that at all events we had improved in the matter of hospital nursing, he cheerfully acknowledged all this. He was greatly pleased with some of the models of sieges, which were picturesque enough, and gave a fresh interest to historical narrative. 'Now this,' he said, pointing to a large glass case, 'is not at all unlike the siege of Platæa, which you will find,' he continued to his trembling listener, 'so wonderfully told in the second book of Thucydides. The difference is that the escalade is of a different kind. The snow is on the ground. The weather is evidently most bitter; the ladders are noiselessly applied; the men are stealing in single line across country.' Mr. Gataker was a scholar: he particularly prided himself on his ancestor's edition of the works of the Emperor Marcus Antoninus. I knew what would please the old man. One day I took him to the Rue de Richelieu, and passing through an archway into the wide, silent court, where a fountain babbles beneath spreading foliage, I took him into the reading-room of the Bibliothèque Impériale, when he was delighted with the studious aspect of the place and its wealth of books, especially delighted when I took him into the manuscript room and placed Pascal's own papers in his hands. To other great libraries I also introduced him, almost unknown by the English in Paris, that of St. Geneviève and the library of the Academy. To those retreats he often stole away when tired of the noise and confusion of the Exhibition. I very much enjoyed one afternoon when I took him to Billancourt, perhaps not the less so because Laura had given us an intimation that it was not impossible that she might be there. I expect Mr. Gataker will greatly rise in the estimation of his churchwardens when he gives in his report of the agricultural implements. He spoke disparagingly of them, however, and said he had seen something as good or better in Berkshire. The surefooted Pyrenean horses interested him, as also did the Arabs, though these last were nearly all of mixed breed, chiefly, I imagined, from mental associations connected with their *habitats*. He very much approved of the Norman method of growing fruit-trees, and was hugely pleased when I took him into Levy's and showed him Breteuil's great work on the subject. I showed him, in the department of books, our unique contributions, consisting of everything published in the year 1866, and I gloried in reflecting that some of my own contributions to the field of literature were included in that *omnium gatherum*. Mr. Gataker, who had not thought so very much even of Mr. Tennyson, made some remarks not very flattering to the residue of modern literature, and he unaccountably failed to discriminate my own modest efforts from the herd. He took also a great deal of interest in the cottages. 'It is all very well to call them cottages,' he said, 'but they were only *cottage ornées*. Country curates might live in them, but what I want is something that would suit my Berkshire labourers on fourteen shillings a week.' I am the more particular in speaking of Mr. Gataker, because he was the very soul of kindness, and the other day, meeting me in a state of deep dejection, he made me come down to his Berkshire rectory, and by his good talk and his good port, such as still lingers in some rectorial abodes, he charmed away a considerable portion of a personal wrong and grief.

That wrong and grief related to Laura Griggs. Words can hardly describe my assiduous attentions to the Griggses in general and to Laura in particular. On the fifteenth of August I conveyed them all over Paris. Who but I could have taken them so quickly from the Trocadero to the Barrière du Trône, have showed them the greased poles, the giants and dwarfs, the theatricals, the serpentine lines of ouvriers waiting for the opening of the opera, and the illuminations at the Arche? How cleverly I got up the whole subject of silk worms, to the admiration of Mrs. Griggs, and took them to the Jardin d'Acclimatization, which was in this respect more interesting than the Exhibition. I made them drive in the long evenings by the side of the lake in the Bois, and took them over to the island and refreshed them at the Swiss café near the cascade; I inaugurated them into the pleasing mysteries of our American cousins' sherry cobbler, champagne frappé, and brandy cocktail; I kept them fully up to the mark in the current history of the Exhibition; I saved them from the inconveniences of the raid upon the chairs; I explained to them the competition and duel of the safes, and assured them that if my genial favourite, Mr. Caseley, had been allowed to compete (his trial at the Old Bailey I had witnessed, and his tearful eloquence had profoundly convinced me of his innocence) he must have distanced all the others; I worked through the galleries with them, pointing out to them the famous pictures of bygone years in Trafalgar Square, and tracing, in what I considered a masterly way, the influence of the modern French school on the whole of continental art. Our intimacy prompted me to the hope that I might one day lead Laura as a bride to my ancestral halls, the ancestral halls in this case signifying a small stuccoed dwelling in Pimlico. I was afraid Laura was worldly. One day when we were talking of the threatened failure of silks, and I had expressed a hope that the Cape silk would be better than the Cape sherry, she said she hoped so, as her dresses had cost her eighty pounds already this year, being the present amount of my modest earnings at the bar. Still, I reflected, the ample resources of old Griggs (despite Overend and Gurney) might reasonably cover such an expenditure. I, however, was certainly not prepared the other day, having addressed a letter to Clapham Park of a certain kind to Laura, to receive an answer in the vulgar handwriting of Griggs *père*. That gentleman was pleased to say that, from the obtrusive nature of my attentions in Paris he was not unprepared for such a communication, but that I had totally mistaken the nature of his daughter's feelings. I have nothing to add to this bare announcement. The marriage mart is set up not only in Belgravia but in the Eden-like groves of Clapham Park. If it was not for Gataker's port I should turn desperate and keep a pike.

Drawn by Florence and Adelaide Claxton.]

ST. VALENTINE'S DAY.

[See the Sketch.

ST. VALENTINE'S DAY.

I HAVE long devoted myself to that kind of observation which

. 'with extensive view, Surveys mankind from China to Peru.'

Of course it has fallen to me, in the operation, to remark many an anxious toil and eager strife, as Dr. Johnson has done before me—many a passion of hope and fear, of desire and hate, of ambition and of love. The conclusion of the whole matter —so far, that is, as I am concerned, for I do not wish to commit the old bear to any proposition half so amiable—has been that love is, after all, the master passion, vanquishing honour, laughing at death, and, about this time of year especially, writing innumerable letters. The catholicity of love and of love-making is the only absolute one; and I back it for the only true and genuine circnicon. The memory of St. Valentine is touchingly and appropriately honoured even by those who have no idea of the red-letter days of a Christian calendar. Fluttering Cupids daintily hold in their softest fetters the gallant mandarin who sees the gentle Venus, *hominum Divumque voluptas*, reflected in the adorable and elliptical eyes of his celestial charmer. Dragged along by the silken cords, we behold in our mind's eye the representatives of all populations, from the Patagonian to the Esquimaux, from the Maori to the Fox Islander, from the Hottentot to the extra-civilized races of Europe.

How the impish progeny of the Queen of Love ring out their joyous glee and let fall their tinkling laughter at the heterogeneous but unanimous procession which marshals itself on the artist's brain and peoples his quaint and fertile invention! First with a becoming and national, but only outward, *insouciance*, marches Young England, male and female; after whom, separated only by the elegant natives of the Flowery Land, who have been introduced already, proceed, with more outward demonstrations of affection, the representatives of a rather more elderly England. The drill-sergeant has fallen back upon the once despised glories of the goose-step, and seems to rejoice in parading the affection of his well-preserved elect. Follows an Arcadian, sentimentally haranguing his lady-love in the chastely-ornamental style of Claude Melnotte, and eloquently descanting about that chateau of his that, on the shore of some lake in lovely Spain, towers up into the eternal summer. Merrily, and taking pleasure pleasantly, trips to dance-music the gay army subaltern of *la grande nation*. Then a nondescript pair, whose passion is that of romance and disguise, who exchange the ever-fresh and kindling vow in the worn-out language of the formal past, and tread meanwhile a stately measure. Follow a crest-fallen couple who have dared the impious experiment of electing friendship to the place of love, one of whom, the spectator rejoices to observe, is justly being tweaked as to the nose for his audacity. The pet god is not more amiable when indulged than vengeful when his patience has been too much or too impudently tried. Next after these rebuked and punished wretches, a lady of Elizabethan time and dignity receives with a gratified hauteur and with a guarded mouth the addresses of the gallant who pays a half-Mephistophelean homage in the shape of a kiss on the coyly-surrendered hand; whilst the knight, whose motto is 'God and the Ladies,' sighs to think of the vows that come between himself and a more particular selection. The squire is happier with his pillioned demoiselle; and Hodge and the grenadier perform to the best of their willing ability the almost double duty which three capricious and capering beauties demand at their hands and hearts. The Elizabethan gentleman in the wake of these is about, we fancy, to contract a *mésalliance;* and the tar walks stoutly off with a lady who must have furtively wandered from the neighbourhood of a court, and who doubtless enjoys the despair of the barrister who in pleading his own cause has become the most unhappy and hopeless of suitors.

All these, however, are the mere phantoms of the artist's brain; but what shall we say of the fortunate pair whose forms in all but flesh and blood occupy the centre of his ornamental lozenge? What shall we say? It is a difficult question for any writer or reader to answer who is conscious of the necessity of remaining true to an allegiance that has been pledged elsewhere. Turn over the page quickly, fair lady or gallant gentleman, unless, indeed, you have the good fortune to be the identical ones represented in all the intensity of pictorial bliss; in which case, as nobly and ungrudgingly as we may, we will wish each of you joy, and pray that every succeeding day may be a renewal of love and a commemoration of this day of St. Valentine.

What memories does not the name of the dear old saint call up—what memories, not all undashed with regret! For, alas! it is so very easy for the best things to degenerate into the worst! As I walk through the streets in these latter days of January I see in the windows of every print-shop flaring and absurd parodies of the tenderest of passions, monstrosities of *inhumanity* intended to burlesque the most sacred and the most universal of mortal or immortal affections—coarse and flaunting vulgarities of form and colour, matched by doggrel verses offensive and ribald beyond the furthest stretch of license. Only here and there amongst the hideous caricatures there is erected some chaste, retiring, and half-exposed altar of Hymen, from which the fumes of incense are with difficulty seen to ascend to the delight of a group of fluttering Cupids, and to the edification of a pair of lovers in the act of blessing each other by the interchange of mutual vows of eternal union and constancy.

My earlier memories of the feast of St. Valentine are of a different order. In a primitive and secluded district, where life seemed to win a solemnity even from its monotony, the claims of the most popular of the saints were not so set at nought. The stately drama was the business of the celebration; the farce, if there was one, was an afterpiece which followed, as the Christmas hilarity followed the morning sermon. I fish up from the inperishable stores of memory the recollection of the mystery that hovered over the actions, the sayings, the inuendoes of my compeers for many days before St. Valentine gave his sanction to those hearty declarations which it were a forlorn hope to suppose could be quite anonymous. The kind of valentine I best remember in those days was one cut out of paper into many curious patterns, and folded afterwards into as many shapes as the ingenuity of waiters has since devised for metropolitan dinner-napkins. Triangular, oblong, square, diamond, circular, polygonal, worked out by the cunning shears to the similitude of most elaborate lace-work, and made vocal by some quaint and ardent rhyme—such were the bait with which we angled for the favour of our chosen fair, and with which, O rapture! we occasionally succeeded in captivating them for a couple of days. The *arbiter elegantiarum* in these matters, without whom nothing could be done, or at least done well, was a cheerful lady who, having slighted the opportunity of taking that ebb in her affairs which led on to matrimony, devoted much of her genial old maidenhood to the delectation of the youth of both sexes. Her services, her taste, her nimble wit and pliant shears, were called into requisition whenever an assault more determined than usual was to be made on some too-obdurate charmer's heart. I know not where now abides the spirit of that vestal priestess of Venus; whether it haply floats about me as I write these lines, or whether, still incarnate, it initiates the youth of the antipodes —whither, obedient to some noble impulse, she went to end her days— into the same mysteries that, twenty years ago, were so piquant and engaging to the youngsters of my native village. Peace be to her, wherever she may be; yea, peace must be with her as a condition of her benevolent and placid existence.

When the valentine was finished came the task of selecting a 'posie,' a legend, a rhyme of true love, which had to be written round and round inwards until it centred finally in a bleeding heart transfixed by the dart of Love. Let the *blasé* reader try to imagine the ineffable tenderness that welled out in such pathetic words as

* The rose is red, the violet blue,
Carnations sweet, and so are you ;
And so are they that sent you this;
And when we meet we'll have a kiss—
A kiss on the cheek and a kiss on the chin,
And when we meet we'll kiss again.'

To this astounding length did our proposals go. Whether they were ever carried out, the present deponent is in no position to say. Another of these poems began with the lines

'As I lay sleeping on my bed,
I saw a rose and it was red;'

the first of which the philosophical inquirer into valentine literature will be interested in comparing with the

'Quant je suy couché en mon lit,'

which commences one of the numerous valentines of Charles Duke of Orleans, a personage with whom we are inclined to wish our space enabled us to make the reader a trifle better acquainted.

In those days, and in that locality, —which, we may inform the reader, in confidence, was in the neighbourhood of the thriving emporium and fashionable watering-place of Dawsmere — we urchins, wise in our generation according to our lights, passed by the temptations of the penny-post and delivered our love-missives in person. After this manner. When the shades of evening had fully closed in upon the face of nature, and a row of blinded and curtained lights streamed out fitfully upon the straggling street, the adventurous youth arose and sallied forth. His elegant declaration—possibly he would be Don Juan enough to fortify himself with more than one—being duly directed in the best disguise his handwriting could assume, was laid tenderly, silently, and with trepidation of heart against some door behind which his *inamorata* was very likely lurking expectant. One good heavy knock and a scamper of feet in fearful flight; the opening of the door, sometimes all too prompt; the groping for the valentine on the part of the *lovée* and her jealous sisters—these were the circumstances that made illustrious the delivery of each. So far the youngster had proceeded in good faith; but now, after having cooled a little from the fever of doubt as to whether he had been discovered, and as to how his devotion had been received by the idol of his soul, he was at liberty to make fun of the fair to whose charms he was indifferent. His next exploit would be a practical joke. A piece of paper folded up in some form proper to the occasion, and promising as much as if it were veritably sick of love, would be perforated for a piece of string. The sham valentine is laid, as before, on the doorstep; the knocker is thumped as emphatically as before; the retirement as speedy as before, but not to so remote a distance. The operator has only retreated to the further extremity of the string, of which the other end secures the traitorously-folded sheet, when, as before, the door opens. Anxious fingers grope until, in the semi-darkness, they pounce at length upon—the bare, cold ground or the vacant stone. The valentine itself has moved about six inches. ''Twas but the wind.' The eluded fingers try and try again, whilst again and again the wind delights to frustrate their intention of taking possession. Then comes the climax of the joke. Whenever a *grab* has been made at the valentine lying on the ground, a judicious pull from the observing youth has attracted it in his own direction; until the mortified maiden, either at length fairly baffled or fully enlightened, gives up in despair or bridles up in wrath, and closes the door with a bang to a chorus of unmannerly laughter from the associates of her tormentor. A variety of this joke was to draw the 'counterfeit presentment' of a valentine in crayon; in other words, to chalk a parallelogram on the ground before the door. But this was a comparatively tame affair, as there could of course be only one disappointment and one triumph before the mean trick was exploded. I think I have heard of pins being introduced into the valentines to which strings were attached; but this was getting far beyond the pale of fun into that of mischief, if not of wantonness and malice. For myself I will not, because I cannot, confess to a malpractice of this kind; but of all the others I thank a certain Venus of eleven years old—at that time, of course; she is now a Juno and a matron—I have had my share. To-day, alas! concerning valentines I must profess *actum est*, so far, that is, as the *sending* of them is concerned. But no man can bar his door against the dulcet appeal of a double knock; and if the valentines I have had the happiness to receive for the last three years from, I believe, the same faithful and devoted angel, were sent by any one who reads this tattle of mine, there is still time for her to know that I am looking forward to my annual compliment, and that I am open to a declaration which shall not be anonymous. After this candid advertisement of the state of my affections I shall know, if the post office is negligent towards me on the morning of the impending festival, that my fair one is faithless and that I am forlorn. May I be spared the tears and dejection of so chilly a conviction; yet let me rather be neglected than scorned. I would not choose to appear, even to myself, depicted with the ears of Midas, or with the sometime head-dress of 'sweet bully Bottom,' the weaver. So much, kind reader, have I been permitted to say of myself; but I have a few stray jottings to lay before you with reference to our dear old St. Valentine and his world-respected day.

The peripatetic delivery of valentines by the principals, to which I have alluded, presents features analogous to the proceedings which, according to the author of 'Rambles in an Old City,' characterize the eve of St Valentine at Norwich. 'The streets,' says Madder, 'swarm with carriers, and baskets laden with treasures; bang, bang, bang go the knockers, and away rushes the banger, depositing first upon the doorstep some packages from the basket of stores; again and again at intervals, at every door to which a missive is addressed, is the same repeated, till the baskets are empty. Anonymously St. Valentine presents his gifts, labelled only "With St. Valentine's love," and "Good-morrow, Valentine." Then within the houses of destination, the screams, the shouts, the rushings to catch the bang-bangs; the flushed faces, sparkling eyes, rushing feet to pick up the fairy gifts; inscriptions to be interpreted, mysteries to be unravelled, hoaxes to be found out; great hampers, heavy, and ticketed "With care, this side upwards," to be unpacked, out of which jump little live boys, with St. Valentine's love to the little ladies fair; the sham bang-bangs, which bring nothing but noise and fun, the mock parcels that vanish from the doorstep by invisible strings when the door opens; monster parcels, that dwindle to thread-papers denuded of their multiplied envelopes, with fitting mottoes, all tending to the final consummation of good counsel, "Happy is he who expects nothing, and he will not be disappointed." It is a glorious night; marvel not that we would perpetuate so joyous a festivity.'

In Devonshire the peasants believe that if they go to the porch of a church, and wait there till half-past twelve o'clock on the eve of St. Valentine's day, with a quantity of hempseed in their hands, and at the time above mentioned, scatter the seed on either side, repeating these lines—

'Hempseed I sow, hempseed I mow,
She (or he) that will my true love be,
Come rake the hempseed after me,'

his or her true love will appear behind, in the act of raking up the seed just sown, in a winding-sheet. In some parts of Norfolk this superstition appears modified in time and purpose. It is there a part of the practices on the eve of St. Mark (April 25) to sow the hempseed in the expectation that it will be mown by the sheeted ghosts of those who are to die that year, marching in grisly array to the parish church. And the rake of the Devonshire spectre is replaced by the scythe of the ghostly Norfolkman. A more pleasant and a more strictly valentine use is made of a variety of the same ceremonial at Ashborne, in Devonshire. There, if a young woman wishes to divine who her future husband is to be, she enters the church at midnight, and, just as the clock strikes twelve, begins to run round the building, repeating, without break or intermission, the following formula:—

> 'I sow hempseed, hempseed I sow,
> He that loves me best,
> Come after me and mow.'

And when the young lady has thus performed the circuit of the building a dozen times without stopping, the figure of her lover is supposed to answer to the gentle invocation, and follow her.

These are Old World superstitions, and we are not to look for them in the New. But in America St. Valentine is popular, and would seem to be turned to a direct practical advantage in the way of initiating the process of courtship and of facilitating the process of matrimony. Of course, in a great country that licks creation, and is just now reposing and 'recuperating' after licking itself; where marriages are cooked up in a short railway trip, and performed by some zealous and opportune clergyman *in transitu*; where railway companies attach 'bridal chambers' to excursion trains as a part of their regular furniture; and where enterprising couples plight their troth and endow each other with all their worldly goods in a balloon—in such a country it is no great marvel if there should be some truth in the hymeneal puff of an advertisement like the following, culled from a 'Worster Democrat' issued in early February a few years ago:—

'The great increase in marriages throughout Wayne Co. during the past year is said to be occasioned by the superior excellence of the

VALENTINES

sold by George Howard. Indeed, so complete was his success in this line, that Cupid has again commissioned him as the "Great High Priest" of Love, Courtship, and Marriage, and has supplied George with the most complete and perfect assortment of " Love's Armor" ever before offered to the citizens of Wayne County. During the past year the " Blind God" has centred his thoughts on producing something in the line far surpassing anything he has heretofore issued. And it is with "feelinks" of the greatest joy that he is able to announce that he has succeeded.

'HOWARD HAS GOT THEM!

'To those susceptible persons whose hearts were captured during the past year, George refers, and advises others to call on them, and find them on their way rejoicing, shouting praises to the name of Howard. The "blessings" descend unto even the third and fourth generations, and it is probable that the business will go on increasing year upon year, until Howard's valentines will be a "household word" throughout the land. The children on the house-tops will call to the passers-by, shouting

"HOWARD'S VALENTINES!"

while the cry is echoed from the ground, and swelling over hill and vale, reverberates the country through.

'Remember that the only regularly-authorized dispenser of Cupid's goods is

GEORGE HOWARD,

two doors East of the American House, Worster, O.

'☞ Orders by mail promptly attended to. Prices range from six cents to five dollars.

'VALENTINES ! ! !

'A large and splendid assortment of valentines, together with all the necessary fixings, for sale wholesale and retail, at the New Column Building.

'J. H. BAUMGARTEN & Co.

'*Worster, Feb.* 3, 1853.'

'VALENTINES.—Behold, St. Valentine's Day is coming, and all are seeking for messages to be despatched under cover of this Saint to friend or foe. They are provided of all kinds, styles, and varieties, ready for use. The turtle-dove kind, with its coo! coo! the sensible sentimental, the cutting and severe, and, in short, everything that can be required. Just call on George Howard or J. H. Baumgarten & Co., and you can be suited to a T.'

Does the curious though hazily-informed reader wish at this stage of our progress to suggest a question as to who St. Valentine was? That is a question to which, thanks to the 'Acta Sanctorum' and Alban Butler's 'Lives of the Saints,' an answer is tolerably easy and precise. 'Valentine was a holy priest in Rome, who, with St. Marius and his family, assisted the martyrs in the persecution under Claudius II. He was apprehended, and sent by the Emperor to the Prefect of Rome, who, on finding all his promises to make him renounce his faith ineffectual, commanded him to be beaten with clubs, and afterward to be beheaded, which was executed on the 14th February, about the year 270. Pope Julius I. is said to have built a church near Ponto Mole to his memory, which for a long time gave name to the gate now called Porta del Popolo, formerly Porta Valentini. The greatest part of his relics are now in the church of St. Praxedes. His name is celebrated as that of an illustrious martyr in the Sacramentary of St. Gregory, the Roman Missal of Thomasius, in the Calendar of F. Fronto, and that of Alla'ius, in Bede, Usuard, Ado, Notker, and all other martyrologies on this day. To abolish the heathen's lewd, superstitious custom of boys drawing the names of girls, in honour of their goddess, Februata Juno, on the 15th of this month, several zealous pastors substituted the names of saints in billets given on this day.' To this we would only enter the single caveat that the *true* relics of St. Valentine are, in a beatified state, at this present moment flaunting in unnumbered stationers' windows, and waiting to be scattered abroad to the four winds of heaven on the wings of every post. St. Francis de Sales, a bishop and prince of Geneva, who died in 1622, and was canonized in 1665, to whom we are inclined, for the sake of his devout treatise on 'Practical Piety,' to forgive everything but this, was one of the 'zealous pastors' who, to use the words of Alban Butler, 'severely forbade the custom of valentines, or giving boys, in writing, the names of girls to be admired and attended on by them: and, to abolish it, he changed it into giving billets with the names of certain saints to honour and imitate in a particular manner.' It is too heartrending to contemplate the disappointment of the ingenuous youth who, hoping to receive the likeness or the name of the blooming Mariana or the saucy Julietta, received instead the effigies of some musty and dyspeptic ascetic at loggerheads with the devil—some Antony of the Desert, or some Dunstan of the Tongs.

In the early part of last century it was the custom for young folks in England and Scotland to celebrate a little festival on the eve of St. Valentine's Day. 'An equal number of maids and bachelors,' says Misson, a traveller of veracity and discernment, 'get together; each writes their true or some feigned name upon separate billets, which they roll up and draw by way of lots, the maids taking the men's billets, and the men the maids'; so that each of the men lights upon a girl that he calls his *valentine*, and each of the girls upon a young man whom she calls hers. By this means each has two valentines; but the man sticks faster to the valentine that has fallen to him than to the valentine to whom he has fallen. Fortune having thus divided the company into so many couples, the valentines give balls and treats to their mistresses, wear their billets several days upon their bosoms or sleeves; and this little sport often ends in love.'

The great Pepys has some quaint and picturesque particulars of his valentine experience. We copy the following entries from his 'Diary':

'Valentine's Day, 1667. This morning came up to my wife's bedside (I being up dressing myself) little Will Mercer, to be her valentine, and brought her name written upon blue paper in gold letters, done by himself, very pretty; and we were both well pleased with it. But I am also this year my wife's valentine, and it will cost me 5*l*.; but that I must have laid out if we had not been valentines.

'February 16. I find that Mrs. Pierce's little girl is my valentine, she having drawn me: which I was not sorry for, it easing me of something more that I must have given to others. But here I do first observe the fashion of drawing mottoes as well as names, so that Pierce, who drew my wife, did draw also a motto, and this girl drew another for me. What mine was, I forget; but my wife's was, "Most courteous, and most fair," which, as it might be used, or an anagram upon each name, might be very pretty.' Pepys tells us also that the Duke of York, being on one occasion the valentine of the celebrated Miss Stuart, afterwards Duchess of Richmond, 'did give her a jewel of about 800*l*.; and my Lord Mandeville, her valentine this year, a ring of about 300*l*.'

But we meant to have anticipated another question on the part of the benevolent reader. St. Valentine being such as he was, and not a bishop who immortalized the day by writing a love-letter upon it—as we were in very early youth given mistakenly to understand by a heresiarch of a nursemaid—how comes his name to be used as a cover for all the love-doings that take place under the quoted sanction of his name and authority? This has already been vaguely explained in the quotation from Alban Butler. But we may say ten more words about it; and these words we choose to say by deputy of the author of a small paper entitled 'The true story of St. Valentine,' which appeared in the 'Churchman's Family Magazine' for February of last year. 'In ancient Rome there was, about the middle of February in each year, held the public festival called Lupercalia, which was given in honour of the Lycæan Pan. One of the numerous ceremonies at this pagan festival was to put the names of young women into a box, from which they were drawn by the young men, as chance directed; and as in those days auguries were thought much of, and exercised great influence over the minds of the superstitious Romans, the girl whose name was thus drawn by lot from the box was considered as a person very likely to become the future wife of the drawer. As a good deal of barbarous and licentious conduct was often the result of this ceremony, the zealous fathers of the early Christian Church used every possible means in their power to eradicate these vestiges of pagan superstitions. The names of saints instead of these girls were placed upon the billets, and that saint which each drew was to be his tutelary guardian during the following year, and as the Lupercalia was, as we have already mentioned, held about the middle of February, they appear to have chosen St. Valentine's Day whereon to celebrate their reformed festival. The exertions of the priests were not altogether barren of good results, for although St. Valentine's Day is a day peculiarly devoted to love affairs, its festivities are no longer associated with the pagan aspect which called forth the righteous ire of the good Fathers of the Church; a result for which we ought to be truly thankful, and one which is a striking example of the good work which Christianity is ever doing. It has not abolished the custom, but purified it. It has taken away the old heathen coarseness and licentiousness, but has left unchanged the play of human feeling and affection; true-hearted lovers, instead of being afraid of their newly-discovered emotions, may have reason to congratulate themselves that they are under the tutelage of so good and noble a saint as Valentine of Rome.'

S. St. M.

CANINE CELEBRITIES.

*'I am his highness' dog at Kew;
Pray tell me, sir, whose dog are you.'*

WHOSOEVER'S dog you, gentle reader, may be, I, the gentle writer, am, for the nonce, M. Emile Richebourg's devoted dog and ardent admirer. That gentleman has had the patience—no, he has allowed himself the pleasure—of putting together a bulky volume, entitled, 'Histoire des Chiens Célèbres,' full of all sorts of stories about all sorts of dogs. He has been dog-fishing on an enormous scale, and his net has hauled to shore an extraordinary variety of canine prey. It is to be hoped that some publisher will, with his permission, present us with the entire work in an English dress. A great many of the dogs are quite new to us. Nevertheless, there are dogs historical, biblical, and classical; serio-comic, melodramatic, tragical, and farcical dogs; dogs political, domestic, and mendicant; every dog, in short, you can imagine, and a great many more; for after reading M. Richebourg's amusing compilation, you will confess that with them, as often occurs with the human race, truth is strange—stranger than fiction.

In turning over his well-filled pages, to select a short example or two, the choice is rendered difficult by his immense store of anecdotic wealth. Which dog shall I first take by the paw to introduce to the British public? Shall it be a lady or a gentleman? a puppy, or a dog advanced in years? a terrier, a turnspit, a coach-dog, or a mastiff? At the present moment, the weighty decision may almost be left to chance; for one of the consequences—perhaps I ought to say one of the premonitory symptoms—of the shooting season is, that men's minds are turned to dogs in general, to pointers and retrievers in particular.

I will therefore ask my sporting readers if they ever had, and what they would do were they ever to have, a dog in the guise of Athos the Terrible—a creature never to be forgotten; although canine celebrity, like human, varies in its kind and quality?

Athos (notorious as 'The Red Dog' throughout the whole arrondissement of Melun) never knew his parents. His mother abandoned him to the care of a goat, who first suckled him, and then discarded him by means of vigorous thrusts with her horns. His father, an incorrigible poacher, appears to have suffered the penalty of the law before he could lick his infant son. At the present writing, Athos is two years old, having been born in Paris on the 15th of June, 1865. Height, twenty inches; hair, carroty red; nose, sharp; chin, round; countenance, angular. Personal peculiarity, a habit of breaking and smashing everything.

In due time, Athos was put out to board and lodge with a gamekeeper, who taught him to find, to point, and to fetch, for twenty francs per month, or two hundred and forty francs per annum. The pupil soon gave signs of promise. In a fortnight he could find a hen in the poultry-yard, catch it at the hencoop, and fetch it to the kennel, where he discussed it in company with a couple of bandy-legged terriers.

'Good!' said the keeper, when he beheld the feathers with which the Red Dog had softened the straw of his bed. 'I think I shall be able to make something of this fellow.'

He at once made out Athos's bill for the month:—

	francs.
Board and instruction during March	20
Hen killed	3
Collar torn	1
Leash broken	1
Medical attendance for indigestion after killing the hen	5
Total	30

The months of April, May, June, July, and August followed, with like results; that is, the Red Dog, making daily progress, added pigeons to hares, ducks to pigeons, and rabbits to ducks. The gamekeeper had never had a boarder so little particular in his choice of food.

On the 4th of September, the day before the opening of the shooting season, Athos's master, Monsieur H——, a rising young doctor with a limited practice, came to fetch him. The teacher brought him out in triumph.

'Mon-ieur,' he said, 'you have got there a most wonderful dog. I shall be curious to hear of his performances.'

'Does he point well?'

'Nothing to boast of. He dashes off in fine style; but he listens to nothing, will have his own way, flushes the game a hundred yards off, runs after it a mile, and then comes down upon the other dogs like a thunderbolt. A good creature, nevertheless; keen nose, sweet temper; all you want.'

'How does he find?'

'Very tolerably. But he is sometimes before you, sometimes behind you, sometimes to the right, sometimes to the left; never within gunshot, and often not within earshot. But a good creature, sharp-eyed, sure-footed, keen-nosed, sweet-tempered; all you want.'

'But I hope, at least, that he can fetch?'

'Whatever you like; hares, rabbits, pheasants, partridges; only he brings the hares and rabbits in quarters and the partridges in halves. But an excellent creature, capital teeth, fine scent, sweet temper; you want nothing more.'

'I can shoot with him, then?'

'Certainly. Here is his little bill.'

francs.
Six months' board and paternal care, at 20 francs per month, as agreed. . . 120
16 hens killed, at 3 fr. 48
4 ducks ditto, at 3 fr. 12
6 pigeons ditto, at 1 fr. 6
18 rabbits ditto, at 3 fr. 54
2 fat geese ditto, at 4½ fr. 9
3 neighbours' cats ditto, at 5 fr. 15
Crockery broken 45
Sheets, napkins, and towels torn and devoured 120
Children bitten, gendarmes insulted, rural policemen scared 100
Total 529

'Five hundred and twenty-nine francs!' exclaimed Monsieur H——, frightened out of his wits. 'Why, the sum is perfectly exorbitant.'

'Not a sou too much. Only keep your dog a fortnight, and you will see whether I have overcharged a single item.'

'Athos must be a confounded thief, then—a thorough brigand!'

'Not at all. He's only young; fond of play. He kills right and left; he plunders; he devours. But he's almost a puppy; he'll grow steadier with age. A good creature, sweet-tempered; the very thing for you.'

Monsieur H—— paid the money with a half-suppressed sigh, and started for the farm over which he was to shoot next day in company with a few select friends and Athos the Terrible.

The night passed quietly enough. The only serious discussion the Red Dog had was with the house-dog, the shepherd's dog, the lap-dog, and the eight pointers, his future companions. The whole was summed up in a few torn ears and an administration of the whip by a waggoner, whose hand was as heavy as his slumbers were light. Next morning, at seven, the sportsmen, after swallowing a cup of café-au-lait, which was to support them till eleven, and Athos with a capon on his conscience, which enabled him to wait for the first wounded hare, ranged themselves in battle array.

The first shot was fired at a covey of partridges immediately after entering a field of beetroot. A bird fell at Athos's nose; he looked at it disdainfully, and set off in chase of the rest of the covey. Unluckily, it kept up on the wing until it reached the Marquis de Bonton's property. Athos, caring little for such trifles, followed it with all the strength of his legs and his lungs.

'Hang the dog! Here, Athos!' and other cries, burst forth from the exasperated gunners.

The noise attracted the marquis's gamekeeper, who whistled the dog to come to him. But Athos, taught by experience that a keeper's whistle is often the precursor of his whip, stared at the whistler and continued the chase, as if the Département of Seine-et-Marne had contained neither a keeper nor a marquis. Nevertheless, the stoutest sinews will tire. After having his run, Athos thought fit to rejoin the sportsmen. As he sauntered up in one direction, the marquis's keeper stalked forward in the other.

'Monsieur,' he said, politely, uncovering first his badge of office and then his head, 'I am very sorry for what has happened, for you have certainly there a most wonderful dog. But we have a painful duty to perform. You will receive tomorrow a summons for trespass. Good morning, Monsieur. I wish you luck.'

'A nice beginning!' muttered poor H——.

'If you wish it to go on better,' said one of his friends, 'I advise you to fasten Athos to your game-bag behind you. Here's a capital strap. If it breaks, I will pay for all the mischief he does.'

The advice was found good. A minute afterwards, Athos and his master were a semi-attached couple, entertaining about the same mutual affection as a constable and his prisoner. They set off again to continue their sport.

'Parbleu!' said H——; 'it was the best thing I could do. Gently, Athos, there's a good dog. I've got him, however. Go at them, now, all you like.'

Telling Athos to 'go at them,' was like telling a thief to steal. He did go at them so well that he upset his master, and got loose by tearing the game-bag to which he was fastened. He then celebrated his liberty by a zig-zag steeplechase, in the course of which he did not leave even a lark upon the ground.

'I have had enough of it for to-day,' said H——. 'You will find me at the farm. Perhaps you will keep an eye on Athos.'

Before entering the house, he thought it prudent to discharge the left barrel of his gun, which he had not fired. He took aim at an apple, and pulled the trigger. The apple did not fall, but the barrel burst. A handful of earth had plugged the mouth of the barrel when the Red Dog had thrown him down on the ground.

At noon the sportsmen returned to luncheon. The Red Dog led the way, seizing, as he entered, a fine roast fowl, breaking the dish, spilling the gravy over the farmer's wife's new dress, and upsetting a maidservant laden with a basket of eggs.

'A pretty piece of business!' exclaimed the farmer's wife. 'If people have no better dogs than that, the best thing they can do is to leave them at home. The next time the Red Dog sets foot in here the house will be too hot to hold him.'

'The dog will be my ruin,' H—— said to himself, turning as red as a new-boiled lobster. 'If this goes on, I shall have to leave the country. I must really take some decisive step.'

With infinite trouble he caught the Red Dog; then he bound him hand and foot; then he chained him to an iron staple inside the box of his dogcart, which he double-locked, and fastened outside with an additional bolt. In this way he reached home without much further unpleasantness. But while his friends were counting their game, he made a little estimate, for his own edification, of what Athos had cost him up to that moment:—

	francs
Keeper's bill for board and training	529
Capon for Athos's breakfast	4
Summons for trespass, &c., &c.	40
Mending torn game-bag	3
Gun burst	300
Roast fowl, for dinner	4
Dish broken	3
Replacing merino dress spoiled by the spilt gravy	60
Basketful of eggs broken	5
Total	948

A fortnight passed without H——'s friends hearing any news of him or of his dog. One of them at last received the following note:—

'MY DEAR CHARLES,

'You know how I hate that fellow Lejeune, and the cause of my hatred. You are aware that he beguiled away my first patient, and persuaded the woman I loved to marry him. I swore to be revenged, and I have kept my word. I have presented him with Athos; he accepts the Red Dog.

'Ever yours, in delighted haste,
'HENRI H.'

Of the ingenious atrocity of this mode of vengeance it is needless for us to say a word.

Our next portrait is that of a drawing-room dog; and as everybody thinks his own dog the best, the dearest, the most interesting in the world, M. Emile Dumont (cited by M. Richebourg) shall present *his* favourite himself.

Bianchino (the diminutive of the Italian word, bianco, 'white') is a Spitzberg dog, a race very largely kept in Russia, which was introduced to France at the time of the invasion—the only fault with which it can be reproached. In winter, Bianchino is a shaggy lion; in summer, he is shorn close, poodle fashion: he is then the drollest-looking creature in the world. Brought up and educated by Captain F——, a retired cavalry officer, he is consequently subjected to strict military discipline. Any infraction of the rules is followed by punishment.

'Ah, Bianchino! you have committed a fault,' is said to him in such a case. 'Go to prison, sir. Consider yourself arrested for one, two, or three days.'

At this order Bianchino droops his head, tucks his tail between his legs, and walks off to one of the corners of the room. There he stands on his hind legs, up against the wall, with his back turned to the company, and remains there until set at liberty; that is, until his master has counted, with intervals of silence more or less long, 'one,' 'two,' or 'three,' according to the gravity of the offence.

Bianchino is very fond of the captain's horse. He frequently visits him in the stable, which is shared with another horse belonging to a friend. These horses are attended to by different grooms, and receive different rations of food. Now the companion horse is allowed carrots, which the captain's is not; and the deprivation is especially tantalising, because the aromatic roots are piled within sight and smell in a corner of the stable.

It was found that this heap diminished rapidly, more rapidly, indeed, than it fairly ought. By careful watching it was discovered that Bianchino was the author of the theft. He thought it hard that his master's horse should not fare so well as the other did, so he pulled the carrots out of the heap one by one, and carried them to his friend, who munched them without scruple.

Bianchino feigns death admirably. At a pretended sword-thrust or a pistol-shot, he falls to the ground, stretches himself out, and remains motionless until the bugle, like the trump of judgment, sounds his resurrection, and gives the signal for resuming his frolics. This, however, is only a souvenir of what he witnessed on the field of battle; for, after serving in the army, he retired on half-pay at the same time as the captain did.

Bianchino dances and waltzes to perfection. At the word of command, rising on his hind legs, he follows the evolutions of his master's hand, which is provided with a lump of sugar. He circles round the room, revolving on his own axis, and keeping time to music when played to him, after which he is rewarded with the sugar. If, however, it is offered to him with the left hand he draws back with offended dignity; but as soon as the morsel is made to change hands he seizes it at once, and makes quick work of it.

In society we are sometimes troubled with visitors who to their other infirmities add the bad habit of leaving doors open behind them. On such occasions Bianchino rushes at the door, and does not rest until the bolt has caught the staple.

Bianchino has also had his fabulous adventures. He went to school, it seems, like you and me. The myth originated thus: He had gone through his performances before a numerous audience. The children of the party laughed till they cried. A curly-headed rogue went up to Captain F., and asked, 'Was it you, Monsieur, who taught him all this?'

'Oh dear no! 'twas his schoolmaster.' Then, addressing the juveniles collectively, he added, 'You see, my young friends, the result of good conduct and perseverance. While still a puppy, Bianchino carried off all the prizes at the Dogs' Academy. Now that his education is complete, instead of being a pupil he has become a teacher.'

The children, mystified, opened their eyes.

'He now gives lessons,' continued Captain F.

'Does he charge dear for them?' one of the young folk inquired.

'That depends; Bianchino has his favourites.'

Upon which the child, turning to his father, said, 'Oh, papa, it would be so nice if you would let him give my dog Blacko some lessons.'

In spite of all which brilliant success, Bianchino's existence was not unclouded. He had a rival—a rival preferred to himself, who put his nose quite out of joint. One day there came to town a little newborn babe. Great was the joy of the delighted parents. The days were not long enough to fondle the child in; the dog was neglected and pushed aside. He growled inwardly as he crouched beneath the cradle. He wept, he groaned, he ground his teeth at the sight of the caresses lavished on baby. But when he saw the infant toddling from chair to chair, when the smiling infant threw his arms round his neck, all aversion and jealousy disappeared. No longer regarding him as a rival, he patronized him as a protégé. He rolled with him over and over on the carpet; he allowed his hair and his ears to be pulled; and on high days and holidays even acted as hobby-horse, maintaining all the while a certain air of superiority.

Bianchino has his place in the family circle, and his photograph figures in the family album. One day, when the boy was sitting for his portrait, the dog came and lay down at his feet. It is a charming group, all the better for being perfectly natural and unaffected.

There are dogs who are almost public characters. Toto, for instance, a white poodle of the purest breed, belonged to a Parisian café-keeper. As neat in person as lively in temper, he was the favourite not only of the master and his men but of all the customers who frequented the establishment. But besides his mere external graces the poodle rendered important service by performing errands entrusted to him. Every morning, carrying the basket in his mouth, he went to fetch the rolls at the baker's. He would make five or six journeys, if necessary, not only without the slightest complaint, but also with the strictest integrity. True, Toto fared sumptuously every day, but the rolls he carried were very tempting.

One morning, as usual, Toto delivered the basket of rolls to his mistress. She counted them: one was missing. The idea of suspecting Toto's honesty never once entered her head. She said to herself, 'The baker has made a mistake.' A waiter was sent to mention the circumstance. 'It is possible,' said the baker, giving the man a roll to make up for the one deficient. 'I did not count them myself; but you may tell your mistress that we will see that all is right to-morrow.'

The next day there was again a roll too few. Again they went to the baker's to complain.

'I counted the rolls into the basket myself,' he said, rather angrily; 'so I am sure they were right. If your poodle is a glutton it is not my fault.'

This speech plainly accused Toto of theft; and appearances, unfortunately, were much against him. Nevertheless his mistress persisted in expressing her doubts, so convinced did she feel of Toto's innocence. She decided, however, to have him secretly followed, in order to catch him in the fact if really guilty.

The next day a waiter, placed in ambuscade, saw him go to the baker's, and leave it with his basket full. Then, instead of taking the direct road home, he turned off by a side-street. The waiter, curious to learn the meaning of this manœuvre, watched him into a courtyard, where he stopped before a stable-door which had a loophole at the bottom, to allow cats to go in and out. The waiter then saw him set the basket down, gently take out a roll, and present it at the cat-hole, where another dog's mouth instantly received it, as if an animal imprisoned there were awaiting its accustomed pittance. That done, Toto took up his basket, and trotted off home as fast as he could.

The waiter, on questioning the portress, was informed that in the stable there was a bitch who had littered only three days ago; and it was exactly for the last three days that the number of rolls brought home was short by one.

On returning he related to his mistress and the customers present what he had seen and what the portress had told him.

'Capital!' exclaimed the lady. 'Bravo, Toto! Good dog! Our hearts would be considerably harder than yours if we treated such conduct as a crime.' She consequently ordered that Toto should have full liberty of action in the disposal of the rolls.

Toto, therefore, using his discretion, continued for a certain time the same allowance to the lady in the straw; and then, when she began to wean her pups, he honestly brought home, as heretofore, the exact number of rolls delivered to him by the baker.

Our next dog answers to the name of Diamond; not the Diamond whose destruction of mathematical papers, so calmly borne by the philosopher Newton, is an instance of canine carelessness, but a far better dog, though of minor celebrity, who has been saved from oblivion by M. Philibert Audebrand.

'Viscount, you engaged me for the third quadrille,' said the Marquise de Servay, a rich young widow who was giving her first ball after throwing off her weeds.

'I cannot deny it, Madame,' replied the Viscount de la Châtaigueraie, a handsome young man, with but scanty resources besides a small estate in the Nivernais and an allowance made him by his uncle, the Archbishop of Bordeaux. The world, however, gave him credit for a good chance of obtaining the widow's hand.

'When the band commenced I looked out for you; but you allowed me to sit here without coming to fetch me.'

'Madame, I cannot deny the fact.'

'The truth is, Viscount, that you like the card-table better than the ballroom; you prefer the Queen of Clubs and the rest of her sisters to keeping your engagement with me.'

'I assure you, Madame——'

'It is quite useless your protesting to the contrary after acting thus. I am sorry that such should be the case; but wretched is the woman who is foolish enough to set her heart upon a gambler. You deserve to be punished, and you shall be, I promise you.'

'At least, Madame, I should like to know the nature of my punishment.'

'Well, sir, it is simply this: I will save you one of my bitch's puppies.' And with a curtsey she left him to join her other guests.

At the present day such a speech would sound vulgar, nay coarse, in a lady's mouth; but in 1782, and at Bourges, the capital of the province of Berri, it was merely a proverbial saying, expressing, in excellent though old-fashioned French, 'I will have my revenge.' During the rest of the evening, seeing that his hostess kept him at a distance, he could not but acknowledge the gravity of his offence, and apprehend the vengeance—a woman's vengeance—with which he had been deservedly threatened.

Nevertheless, a month elapsed without the occurrence of any unpleasant circumstance. La Châtaigneraie, believing that the Marquise bore no more malice than he did himself, supposed that his fault was forgiven or forgotten. He had come, however, to too hasty a conclusion. One January evening, on his return from shooting, Fridolin, his valet, handed him the following letter:—

'DEAR VISCOUNT,

'A promise is as binding as a written engagement. An honest Marquise must keep her word. I said I would save you one of my bitch's puppies. You will receive it a few minutes after the delivery of this. Oblige me by giving him the name of Diamond, which his ancestors have borne with unblemished honour.

'Yours, with sincere compliments,
'THE MARQUISE DE SERVAY.'

La Châtaigneraie had scarcely finished reading the note when a servant entered and presented him with a basket, in which he found a little greyhound pup. He began to swear, feeling himself humiliated and a laughing-stock. The joke, he thought, had been carried too far. The creature was weakly and anything but handsome; so he told his man to tie a stone to its neck, and drown it in the Loire.

'Poor thing,' said Fridolin. 'It is not its fault if Madame amuses herself at your expense. Let me keep it, Monsieur, and bring it up. I will undertake all the trouble myself.'

'Do as you please. If Madame de Servay were but a man! or if she only had a brother to answer for her impertinence!'

This jeer in action galled him deeply. Instead of regarding it as a good-natured mystification, he considered it meant as a proof of disdain. He could not drive it out of his mind; and having heard that India was the real Eldorado, he resolved to solicit the king for a commission, and seek his fortune at Pondicherry.

'Since my suit is repulsed thus scornfully,' he said, 'I will console myself by acquiring wealth.'

A fortnight afterwards he sailed from Marseilles on board the brig 'Duquesne,' bound for the Carnatic.

When the Marquise de Servay heard of his departure, she, in turn, felt exceedingly vexed.

'What nonsense has he taken into his head,' she exclaimed, 'to treat seriously in this way a mere piece of harmless pleasantry? I was fond of him, and was quite prepared to let him see it.'

'Ah, Madame!' said a lady in her confidence, 'there are three things you should never play with—the fire, your eyes, and your affections.'

La Châtaigneraie was absent a couple of years. He fulfilled the mission intrusted to him with great credit to himself. Some English prizes (vessels captured at sea) in which he had a share brought him in two hundred thousand francs, at that time a considerable sum. Then there was his allowance of two thousand crowns a year from the Archbishop of Bordeaux, besides his claim on the royal treasury for his services at Pondicherry; so that he was quite in a position to return to Europe.

He did return, at the beginning of the year 1785, first to Paris, then to Bourges. At any epoch two years are a considerable lapse of time; under the *ancien régime* they were especially so. Nothing is stable here below; and the Nivernais nobleman found many things changed. On presenting himself at one of Madame la Présidente de Morlieu's receptions he heard the news of the neighbourhood. Amongst other things he learned that the pretty Marquise de Servay, tired of waiting, and uncertain whether he would ever come back, had taken to herself one Maurice d'Esgrigny, a sort of small Baron in the Sologne, as a second husband some six months ago, her choice having been guided, gossips said, by his intrepidity as a dancer.

La Châtaigneraie therefore retired to his Nivernais home. After Fridolin, still his only attendant, the first creature who came to meet him was a rough-coated greyhound, a sort of lurcher, with bloodshot eyes, and of not at all a prepossessing appearance; but he wagged his tail to beg for favour, and licked his master's hand in token of affection.

"Ah! I recollect you, ugly brute. You are a reminder of my late mishap,' said the Viscount, lashing him with his riding-whip. 'Go to the devil!'

With a plaintive cry the animal turned round, and crawled back on his belly to his master's feet.

'If I might be allowed to speak,'

said Fridolin, 'I would say a few words in Diamond's favour.'

'Yes, I remember; Diamond is his name.'

'Monsieur doubtless has not forgotten that he gave me permission to bring up the pup. I did so, and have had no reason to repent of it.'

'What is he good for?'

'With Trumeau's (your old keeper's) help, I have made him the best dog in the neighbourhood. He always has his wits about him. He is first-rate in unearthing a fox, starting a roe-deer, and driving a boar. Diamond's courage is extraordinary; he is afraid of nothing, and has teeth of iron. Last winter, when the ground was covered with snow, he fought with and strangled in less than five minutes a wolf that had forced its way into the courtyard. As a trophy I cut off his feet and head, and nailed them to the stable-door. What does Monsieur think of these?'

At the sight La Châtaigneraie could not restrain a smile of approbation. 'As you give him such excellent testimonials,' he said, 'I have no wish to bear malice any longer. There, Diamond, let us make it up,' he added, patting the dog's head, and nothing further passed in the matter for a time.

Some days afterwards the Viscount went out shooting, taking with him the once despised dog. On his way back he said to himself, 'Fridolin is right; there cannot be a better sporting dog. The Marquise, without intending it, has made me a very valuable present.'

Before the week was out La Châtaigneraie had taken the dog completely into favour. When the creature came to caress and be caressed, he would say, 'Good Diamond! You are the best friend I have, for you owe me in spite of my injustice. I'm sure you would defend me at the risk of your life;' and then the dog would bark his assent.

A year afterwards, in the depth of winter, the Viscount, going from Nevers to Avallon, entered, towards the close of day, a woody defile of the Morvan, a hilly country of bad repute. He skirted the forest called the Tremblaye. It was an act either of foolish imprudence or of very determined resolution; for the neighbourhood was notorious for the murders that were almost daily committed there. On so rough and ill-conditioned a road he could not hope to escape an attack by flight, however powerful his horse might be. On the other hand, neither the pistols he carried nor the raw-boned lurcher which ran before him were a sufficient protection against the bands of robbers which then infested the east of France.

Moreover, the Viscount, still fond of play, had lately lost ten thousand francs on his parole, and was now loyally taking it in gold to the winner. Without manifesting apprehension, he nevertheless urged his horse to do his best. 'Patience, Acajou!' he said. 'You'll soon get plenty of oats and hay. Courage, good Diamond! Don't you smell your supper?'

His first intention had been not to halt before reaching one of the intermediate towns between Nevers and Avallon; but as he felt himself oppressed by drowsiness, he changed his plan and hastened his pace, in order to sleep at the Tête-Noire, an inn situated in the middle of the wood. He reached it before very long. Finding the door shut he knocked for admission.

Strangely enough, although the house seemed in a bustle, to judge from the voices and the lights which flashed about in the upper story, he got no answer. The door remained closed.

'Are you all deaf?' he shouted, knocking louder. 'Can't you hear there is some one come to pass the night?'

After a while a window opened. 'Who is there?' inquired the innkeeper, with feigned surprise.

'It's me. Master Pennetier, the Viscount de la Châtaigneraie. I have already told you I want a night's lodging.'

'A hearty welcome to you, Monsieur le Vicomte. Jeanne! George! Why don't you run downstairs and open the door to let the worthy gentleman in? You seem as if you meant to keep him waiting outside all night long.'

Admitted at last, the Viscount could not help expressing his astonishment. 'Master Pennetier, you must be hard of hearing to-day. I knocked at the door at least ten minutes, and yet you were not abed and asleep. What the deuce were you so busy about upstairs there?'

The man forced a grin, and stammered, 'We were busy about—all sorts of things. There is so much to do in an out-of-the-way inn like this. Jeanne, unstrap that knapsack from the saddle; and you, George, take Monsieur's horse to the stable. Give him all the corn he likes to eat.'

The maidservant, to show her obedience to orders, not only took the knapsack indoors, but began to open it and examine its contents, as if arranging them for the traveller's use.

'Stop a minute! not quite so fast!' said the Viscount. 'I'll do that myself, when I want it.' Then imprudently adding, 'There's gold enough there to marry off the ugliest girl in Morvan; and you are too pretty to stand in need of that.'

Jeanne opened wide her little black eyes, and so did Master Pennetier his squinting grey ones.

'Yes,' continued La Châtaigneraie, with the boastful rashness habitual to the gentlemen of that day, 'my knapsack is heavy: you will therefore be good enough to let me have a room that is secure against intrusion.'

'The most secure in the Tête-Noire, Monsieur le Vicomte; although, as for that, all rooms are safe in an honest man's house. George, get the chamber on the first floor ready.' And as George seemed to hesitate, he added, 'Be off with you quickly! Do you think I don't know what suits my customers? And you, Jeanne, give Monsieur his supper.'

They set before him, regretting they had no more, a leg of mutton, some salad, dried fruits and cheese for dessert, with a bottle of excellent Sancerre wine. La Châtaigneraie ate heartily, declaring there was quite enough for him and for Diamond too. It was ten o'clock by his Geneva watch when he rose from table and retired to his bedroom. As he entered he deposited the knapsack in a corner; Diamond went and lay down upon it.

'Just so, good fellow; keep guard there.' Casting a glance round the room, he observed to himself, 'The look of the place is not inviting; but for one night it does not matter much.' He then undressed and got into bed.

Under the influence of fatigue he was about to blow out the candle and fall asleep, when he noticed that the dog had suddenly left his post, walking round the bed and sniffing under it in a singular way.

'What can this mean?' La Châtaigneraie thought. He rose, and felt under the bed, to ascertain the cause. He shuddered involuntarily as his hand touched a human foot—a cold and naked human foot.

During his stay in India he had witnessed, in the character both of actor and spectator, not a few incidents of a startling nature, but he had never met with anything so horrible as this. Doubting whether he were not in a dream or the victim of some frightful hallucination, he took the candle and looked under the bed. It showed him that he was under no delusion. There lay a corpse—the dead body of a man!

Diamond looked into his master's eyes, as if to ask what he should do—bark an alarm or hold his peace.

'Hush! keep quiet!' whispered the Viscount, at the same time, making an effort on himself, he drew the body into the middle of the room.

La Châtaigneraie was really brave when he knew the adversary with whom he had to deal. But what was this mysterious piece of villany? How was he to defend himself in the dead of the night, alone, in an isolated inn? Either the matter was inexplicable, or he was compelled to conclude that the people of the house had committed murder, and that the same fate was reserved for him. He took counsel with himself what to do, what to decide on in such a situation. Flight was impossible; besides, the Viscount was one of those men who never flee.

He dressed himself again.

'But how can I tell,' he thought, 'that there are not ten or a dozen cut-throats assembled in this den? In that case, how can I avoid falling into their clutches? They may come down upon me at any moment. There is no time to lose.'

Summoning all his presence of mind, he made Diamond go back to the knapsack and lie down upon it. Searching round the room, he discovered a secret door in the alcove which contained the bed. He concluded that that was how the murderers entered in order to commit their crimes, in which case it would be unwise to bar it. He therefore put the body into the bed at exactly the place he would have occupied himself; then he extinguished the light, and, armed with his pistols, crept under the bed, lying down on the spot whence he had drawn the body.

There he waited, listening attentively. For an hour he saw nothing but Diamond's eyes, which shone like a couple of burning coals. But very soon after one in the morning he heard the paper which lined the alcove creak; the secret door slowly opened, and in the midst of the darkness a man leaned stealthily forwards over the bed and stabbed the body afresh, repeating his blows several times.

'I must have done his business!' the assassin muttered.

Hardly had the words escaped his lips when Diamond rushed at him, and with his powerful teeth tore his cheek.

'The devil take you!' the murderer growled. 'As soon as it is light I will serve you as I have served your master.' The door then closed and all was silent.

At cock-crow La Châtaigneraie crept out of his hiding-place, with the full determination of quitting the house by some means or other. At daybreak he heard the sound of wheels; they were carriers' carts, whose drivers halted for their morning dram.

'Now is our time, Diamond,' whispered La Châtaigneraie, taking his knapsack and stalking downstairs, making all the noise he could.

'Saddle my horse instantly,' he said to the astonished innkeeper, whose face was tied up in a handkerchief. And he set off on his journey without bidding his crestfallen host farewell.

That very evening the officers of justice came and searched the Tête-Noire inn. Pennetier and his accomplices were sent for trial before the Criminal Court of Dijon. As the innkeeper persisted in denying many of the facts of which he was accused, the Viscount, remembering the legendary story of the Dog of Montargis, said to the magistrate, 'Next to myself, the principal witness is my dog, Diamond, who set his mark upon the murderer's cheek. I demand that he be brought into court.'

The case was considered sufficiently grave for this evidence to be regarded in a serious light. When Diamond was confronted with the prisoner, his eyes flashed fury, he showed his teeth, and if La Châtaigneraie had not held him tight, he would have torn the innkeeper to pieces.

That well-deserved punishment was only deferred. Master Pennetier was condemned to death. Three months after the commission of the offence he was broken on the wheel, alive, in front of the palace of the Dukes of Burgundy.

Diamond became the lion of the neighbourhood, and La Châtaigneraie grew more and more attached to the courageous creature who had so effectually helped him.

'Monsieur le Vicomte,' said Fridolin one day, 'was I not right in begging you to let me keep the dog?'

The question painfully recalled Madame de Servay's joke, as well as what he was pleased to term her treachery.

Meanwhile a storm was brewing, which threatened to sweep over not only all France but the whole of Europe. That storm was THE REVOLUTION, with its train of horrors, its torrents of blood, and its avenging thunderbolts. One of the first pitiless war-cries raised was, 'Down with the châteaux! spare the cottages!'

La Châtaigneraie, who dwelt in an unpretending old manor-house, with a pepper-box tower for its sole fortification, listened to these menaces without alarm. In the first place, because he was brave and capable of defending himself if attacked by a mob; and secondly, because he was greatly beloved and did not know a single enemy. Almost all his neighbours, however, were emigrating. Some, who were going to Germany to take up arms against the promoters of the Republic, urged him to follow their example.

'No,' said the Viscount, quietly but decidedly. 'I respect the feelings and the motives of those who think fit to enter a foreign service as the best way of assisting their king, but I have no intention of doing as they do; neither do I mean to remain at home, to be slaughtered like a sheep one of these days.'

'What will you do, then?'

'I shall follow the advice of a young Breton officer whom I recently met in Paris.'

'His name?'

'The Viscount René-François de Châteaubriand. He recommended me to make a tour in the New World, and remain there till the tempest shall have passed away. It is useless to fight with the elements let loose. When the storm is over I can return to France, and help to reconstruct the ruins of our country.'

'Do you go alone?'

'Certainly not.'

'Whom do you take with you?'

'The best of friends.'

The Viscount whistled. 'Here, Diamond. This way. Show yourself. The day after to-morrow you and I, and Fridolin also, if he likes to come, will start for America, to avoid witnessing what threatens to occur at home.'

THE PRIVATE LIFE OF A PUBLIC NUISANCE.

IT is no uncommon thing with folks of an ingenious turn to make 'capital,' as the saying is, out of what at first sight seems calamity. As, for instance, a friend of mine, an Alpine traveller, and an indefatigable naturalist, whilst on a journey of exploration in his favourite mountainous region, one night retired to his couch exhausted by the fatigues of march and faint for sleep. It was denied him, however. Not that 'Nature's soft nurse' was ill-disposed towards him; not that his conscience was ill at ease; not that he had supped rashly or inordinately. It was because he was wanted for supper. That ravenous monster, the Alpine flea, but meagrely fed through many months on hardy herdsmen and chamois hunters, sniffed his tender carcase, and without even the warning of 'fe-fo-fi-fum,' fell on him from the roof rafters, and commenced his savage and sanguinary repast. A man of common mind and courage would have engaged the enemy until exhausted, and then yielded at discretion. Not so my friend. He struck a light, and calculating his chances of a night's rest, and finding the balance heavily against him, he coolly dressed himself, and unpacking his microscopical instruments, selected and impaled a few of the largest and finest of his tormentors, and passed a pleasant and profitable night in investigating the peculiarities of the form and structure of *pulex irritans*. There is no knowing how much of ingenuity dwells in the human brain till it is pressed between the hard mill-stones of necessity. Before now, despairing captives have beguiled the tedium of dungeon life by a study of the habits and manners of the very rats which at first were so much their horror and aversion.

I have an enemy more tormenting than any flea that ever hopped—more voracious than the rat, inasmuch as he feeds not on my bread and my cheese, but on my brain. I have little mouths to fill, and little feet to cover, and little backs to clothe; I have house-rent to pay, and water-rate; I have to contribute shillings and pounds towards the maintenance of the poor, and the police, and the main drainage; I have to provide against the visit of the income-tax collector; and to meet these various demands, being a scribbler of the hard-working sort, I am compelled to set my pen dancing over the paper with considerable rapidity and perseverance. And I am very willing to do so. I am willing to sit down in the morning early as any tailor or cobbler, and make my hay while the sun shines. But this my tormentor forbids. He, too, has hay to make while the sun shines. He makes his hay out of my green hopes, sapped and withered; he grinds my brain to make him bread. He bestrides my sober pen, all sudden and unexpected, as it is plodding industriously over the paper, and sets it jigging to the tune of 'Hop Light Loo' or the 'Ratcatcher's Daughter.' He fills the patient, well-intentioned quill with the jingling idiotcy common in the mouths of banjo-playing, bone-rattling Sambos and Mumbos, and turns the common sense about to be uttered by it into twaddle and profitless nonsense. He breaks into my storehouse of thought and turns its contents topsy-turvy. He seizes my golden hours, and condemns them to a lingering and horrible death, mauling them and pulling them into flinders, and leaving me to make the best I may of the few minutes his monkey mischief has left entire. The name of this blowfly in my larder, this weevil in my meal-jar, is Organ Grinder.

It is, of course, well known to me that, in accordance with a recent Act of Parliament, I am at liberty to set the engine of law in motion to crush the organ man if he annoys me; but there is a power much greater than any Act of Parliament ever passed and backed by it. My tormentor may grin defiance at his arch-enemy, Bass. No less true than paradoxical, the superior power in question consists in a weakness—the weakness inherent in every free-born Englishman, to succour all such as he may find downtrodden and driven to the wall. Why downtrodden is a question which the noble-minded Briton never stops to inquire. It is enough that a poor fellow is down, to enlist for him the Briton's heartiest sympathies. Never mind how richly he may have merited the shoulder hit that laid him low, he has only to groan plaintively as he lies in the mire—to whine a little, and beseech pity, and a hundred hands are stretched forth to lift him up, and a hundred mouths are opened to cry 'Poor fellow!' There is ointment for his bruises in shape of a gathering of money, and he is set on his legs and hailed as a man and a brother. Who did it? A parcel of stuck-up, purse-proud, bloated aristocrats! Why don't you hit one your own size? Hit him again, if you dare. This noble sentiment has been of immense service to the downtrodden organ grinder. The law, acting in behalf of O. G.'s suffering victims, having knocked O. G. down, the highminded but tough-skinned British mob has set him up again, and taken him under its special protection. I have no inclination to dispute its right to do so. It admires organ grinding. To be sure, the fact of its utter indifference to the existence of barrel-organs and hurdy-gurdies before the passing of the Act is calculated to give rise to the suspicion that pig-headed obstinacy may have something to do with it, but there is nothing for certain. The miller who could sleep tranquilly while his mill was clashing and crunching and rumbling, awoke the moment the mill stopped. The mob is the best judge of what suits it. It likes its music full flavoured, and with plenty of grit in it. A weaker quality falls idly on its tympanum. Some animals are so thin-skinned that the titillation of a hair will drive them to madness, whereas the rhinoceros delights to have his hide rasped with the prongs of a pitchfork; but that is no reason why the rhinoceros should not be tickled if he likes it.

So it comes about that the organ

grinder finds in the notice of ejectment that was served on him a new lease. But a few months since he was a skulking, surly wretch, with a heavy tread, a hanging head, and the general air of a felon, hopeless as to this life, and by no means comfortably assured of the next; a broadshouldered muscular, doomed for some monstrous iniquity to tramp the highways and byeways of a foreign land, fettered eternally to a demon of discord—a lunatic Orpheus riding him old-man-of-the-sea-wise, torturing his sensitive ear, and mocking his weariness with 'funny' music worthy of St. George's-in-the Fields, or, at the very least, of Earlswood. A treacherous, lean dog, ready for a halfpenny to mow and grin and show his teeth to win the smiles of little children at the window, and equally ready, should he be rashly informed that the little ones are ill, to haggle and make terms as to his consenting to cease from racking their poor little heads with his horrible din; a worse than ghoule, hunting for sickness that he might make a meal of it, with vulture eyes for sadly drooping window-blinds and muffled knockers, and a keen scent for mercifully-strewn tan, that the wooden leg of his engine of torture may find standing in the midst of it.

Distinguished by such unamiable characteristics, it was impossible to love the organ man; still, seeing him go about so evidently conscious of his own unworthiness, so downcast and depressed, and altogether miserable, your indignation was not unfrequently tinctured with pity, and you had at least the gratification of noting that, however much he plagued and tormented you, he never appeared to get any satisfaction out of the transaction beyond the grudged penny flung to him. But since he has been 'persecuted' the aspect of the case has become altogether altered. The organ grinder is no longer a glum villain serving his term of life as though it were a punishment, and not a privilege. The dull dead log has sprouted green leaves, and become quite a sprightly member of society. True, he has not given up the ghoule business, nor the lean dog business, but now he is a ghoule in a cutaway coat in place of a shroud; the lean dog cocks his ears, and carries his tail with an insolent and defiant curl in it. He is a man and a brother in pursuit of his honest calling. He has music to vend in ha'porths and penn'orths; and if you don't choose to buy, there are plenty of householders in your street that will. Don't put yourself out of the way, my dear sir; don't stand there at your parlour window shaking your head, and frowning, and making threatening gestures; he is not playing for *your* edification; he is playing to the people next door but one; they are his regular customers, and take a penn'orth of music of him every morning as regularly as they take a penn'orth of dog's meat for Mungo. A pretty thing, indeed, that you should presume to order him off just because you don't happen to like music! You might as reasonably prohibit the dog's-meat man from calling at number thirteen because nobody on your premises has an appetite for dog's meat. This is the argument provided for the organ grinder by his noble champions and supporters, and he is not slow to avail himself of it. How can you be out of temper with a poor fellow who knows not a word of the language in which you are abusing him, and therefore cannot retaliate? It is mean, it is cowardly, it is un-English. It would not be surprising if he turned round on you and pelted you with such broken bits of English as he is master of. But he is a good-humoured fellow, and does nothing of the kind; if you shake a stick at him, he replies by thrusting out his tongue, and making a funny face at you. If you appear at your gate and order him off, he is moved to no worse than playfully applying his thumb to the tip of his nose, and twiddling his outstretched fingers. Yah! Go in. Stuff your ears with wool. It will be quite time enough for him to go when he sees you rushing down the street in search of a policeman. Even if you have the good luck to find one in time, and the courage to give the ruffian into custody (which means accompanying the 'charge' to the station-house, and being hooted and chaffed by the organ grinder's friend, the mob, all the way you go), you will probably find the game hardly worth the candle. The prisoner does not know one word of English, explains the interpreter to the magistrate, and was quite unaware that the gentleman wished him to go away. But, says his worship, the gentleman states that he took the trouble to come out into his garden to motion you away. That is true, replies the interpreter, after referring his worship's remarks to the now deeply penitent grinder, but the prisoner misunderstood— he thought that the gentleman was come out to dance.

It may occur to the inexperienced that all this is most unnecessary fuss, the remedy for the alleged grievance being so obvious. The organ grinder is no fool; all he seeks is your penny, and cares not how little he does for it; what, therefore, can be easier than to save your time and your temper by sending him out so paltry a sum with the civil message that you won't trouble him to play. You may be making some sacrifice of principle, it may cause you momentary annoyance to suspect that your enemy grins as he turns from your gate with your penny in his pocket, but look on the other side of the question! The blow-fly banished from your larder, your meal-jar freed from the devouring weevil, your quill rescued from its impish rider, your golden hours round and sound and all your own!

You are right, oh innocent adviser! Cheap, dirt cheap would it be if, on payment of a penny, immunity from persecution might be purchased. It would be a stroke of business on the accomplishment of which we might well be proud if one bought off the whole brigand army at a like figure. But beware of the pitfall! Should you be weak enough to yield that first single penny your doom is sealed. It is merely a hushing fee entitling you to rank amongst the organ man's regular customers. The torturer will now regard himself as regularly engaged, and exactly a week from the time when you committed the fatal error, he will turn up again, his countenance beaming with a smile of recognition as you amazedly look out on him from your window, and he won't budge until he gets his penny. Nor is this all. You are duly reported at the head-quarters of the sworn brotherhood of grinders as another to the long list of victims willing to pay for peace, and for the future no organ or hurdy-gurdy bearer will pass your door without giving you the opportunity for exercising your philanthropy. There is no cure for the evil; organ-grinding has become a settled institution of the country, and as such must be endured.

And having arrived at this conviction comes in the example of the Alpine traveller quoted at the commencement of this paper—of the poor prisoner who beguiled the tedium of incarceration by an examination of the habits and manners of the rats which at first were his horror. Might I not be better employed than to sit moping in my chamber with vinegar rags adorning my throbbing temples because of these Italian rats squealing under my window? Were their habits and customs less interesting than those of the four-legged vermin? Did I know more about one than the other? Decidedly; but the advantage was with the quadrupedal animal. I *do* happen to know something about *mus decumanus*. I know that its hind legs are longer than its front ones, that it has a propensity for burrowing under walls, and that it commonly sits on its hind legs and holds the food it eats in its fore paws. I know that its nature is very cunning; that, acting in concert, rats have been observed to cart off unbroken eggs from a basket, one, acting as 'cart,' lying on his back and cradling the egg between his fore paws, while two other rats, acting as teamsters, have dragged home the 'cart' by its tail. I have heard, and place equal reliance in, the story of the rat that emptied a narrow flask of oil by lowering his caudal appendage into it, withdrawing it, licking it clean, lowering it again, and so on. But I don't know half as much about the organ grinder. That his fore limbs are shorter than his lateral may be assumed, but what about his burrowing? That he *does* burrow is certain, because during certain hours of the twenty-four he, happily, disappears. He must have a home somewhere. He is met at all hours of the day as far away as Highgate, Hammersmith, and Sydenham, but come night wherever he may be, he is invariably found to be turning his steps in a north-westerly direction. However far away, he is rarely seen refreshing himself at an inn; he was never yet known to apply for a bed at the wayside country public-house. It is doubtful if he made such an application whether it would be entertained. If a man on horseback applied for lodging the matter might be easily arranged, the man to his chamber and the horse to the stable; but a man with an organ! They are inseparable. He is an organ man—a man with an organ on his back, as other unfortunates have a lump on theirs—with the difference that the former, for business purposes, admits of being occasionally slewed round to the front part of the man's body. Fancy letting a clean and decent bed to a man with an organ on his back!

Then as to the grinder's family. Has he a wife and children? How do they employ themselves? Are the white-mice boys and the guinea-pig boys, the monkey-boys and the boys with the hurdy-gurdies the organ grinder's children? Are those his daughters who go about with a silk handkerchief about their heads, singing and playing on a tambourine? Where is his wife? Is she still to be found working in the vineyards of the sunny South, or does she reside with her 'old man' on Saffron Hill, occupying a snug little room, ironing the grinder's shirts and mending his stockings and preparing something comforting and savoury for the poor fellow's supper, when at midnight he stumps in from Sydenham or Brentford? Does Mrs. Grinder ever go out washing or charing to eke out her husband's earnings? What were his earnings? Did the little Grinders go to school? Was it all work and no play with father Grinder? or did he occasionally take his pipe and his pint and seek diversion like another working man?

I had frequently observed that the organ grinder ceased from his persecution earlier on Saturday than all the other days of the week. On other evenings he was to be heard as late as ten and even eleven o'clock; but on Saturdays, even though you wanted an organ-man, it would be difficult indeed to find one after four or five o'clock in the afternoon. How was this? Was Saturday evening an 'off-time' with the grinder? Was he a patron of the Saturday half-holiday movement? If so, how did he profit by the indulgence? Did he belong to some corps of volunteers? not likely. Did he make one of four for a quick pull up the river? He could not well accomplish such a feat without divesting himself of that peculiarly blue corderoy jacket of his; and the sight of an organ-man in his shirt sleeves is one that never yet met human gaze. Did he take a cheap excursion ticket and go to the Isle of Wight or Margate? What! without his organ? Preposterous. How *did* he spend the only work-a-day evening he could spare from drudgery? The only way to set the question at rest was by personal investigation. No time like the present, which happened to be a Saturday afternoon.

Putting on a slouchy coat and a slouchy cap, I at once set out for Saffron Hill, making it my business to call on my road for an artist friend whose sketches have often delighted the readers of this magazine. My pretence for desiring his company was that there was a probability of his finding a picture worth sketching in some one of the many strange places I purposed taking him to; but my main object in soliciting his company was that I might be benefited by his protection in the event of my being forced into doubtful company—our artist being a man of extraordinary size and muscular development.

It was a lonely evening for such a wild-goose chase as was ours—dark over head, miry under foot, and drizzling wretchedly of rain. I call it a wild-goose chase, and it was little less, for beyond the popularly-accepted belief that the home of the organ grinder was 'somewhere in the neighbourhood of Hatton Garden,' we were in utter ignorance of the abiding place of the individual of whom we were in search. Hatton Garden, as the reader is possibly aware, is a long and wide street opening from the crown of Holborn Hill.

At 7 p.m., the darkness and the drizzling rain nothing abated, we arrived at Hatton Garden, and diligently perambulated that lengthy and retired street from this end to the other, but either in or out of harness not a solitary organ man did we meet. I say out of harness on my companion's account, not mine own; he was quite sure, he said, that he could detect an organ-man even though disguised in the garb of a Quaker. No opportunity, however, for a display of his extraordinary sagacity occurred; and we arrived at the end of Hatton Garden and found ourselves at Hatton Wall, no wiser, as far as the object of our search was concerned, than when we turned out of Holborn.

Hatton Wall is by no means a nice place for a stranger to find himself blindly groping about on a dark February night: indeed, making an allowance of sixty per cent. for time and wealth, I should be inclined to say it was one of the ugliest, if not the most ugly, spots in London. There may be uglier. In one's peregrinations round about London you never know when you have arrived at the worst. I thought I had done so when I first beheld Neal's Buildings in Seven Dials, but was fain to acknowledge my error on an investigation of Brunswick Street, Ratcliffe Highway, and even this—the hideously-renowned Tiger Bay—must, as I afterwards discovered, knock under to Little Keate Street, Whitechapel. Yet it is hard to award the palm, the claim to the supremacy of ugliness being based each on different grounds. Neal's Buildings is nothing worse than the stronghold of Irish squalor, and all manner of filthiness and rags and beggary. The women squat in groups on the squelchy pavement of Neal's Buildings on hot summer days, airily garbed, and with a toothed instrument of horn sleeking their golden tresses, and smoking stumpy pipes, and singing good old Irish songs, and holding cheerful converse with their male friends, some sprawled over the door threshholds, some lounging half out of first and second-floor windows, their shocks of fiery hair surmounted by a nightcap, and so full of gaping and yawning as to give rise to the suspicion that they are not yet entirely out of bed. Tiger Bay is less repulsive at first sight; indeed, it is only when night closes in, and the women, turned wild beasts, leave their lairs to prowl abroad and hunt for sailors, and the born whelps and jackals and hyenas in man shape congregate and lurk in washhouses and coal-holes, ready to pounce out on and beat and worry nigh to death the hapless wretch the females of their tribe have lured to the common den, that Brunswick Street appears uglier than its neighbours. Little Keate Street, again, taken as a street, is not particularly ill-looking; and the traveller might innocently enough take it as a promising short cut to eastern parts of the metropolis. Nevertheless it is a terrible street. It is from thence that the midnight burglar sallies with his little sack of 'tools' and his bits of wax candle and his lucifer matches and his life-preserver. These, however, are amongst the better sort of tenants inhabiting Keate Street—fellows who can pay their way handsomely, and being to a man liberal dogs—the stay of any poor wretch of their acquaintance who may stand in urgent need of assistance. Ask the shopkeepers of the neighbourhood—ask the butcher and the cheesemonger concerning his Keate Street customers! If they tell you as they told me when a year or so since it was my business to be making such inquiries, they will say that they live luxuriously. 'It's nothing, bless you,' said the butcher, 'for them to order a quarter of lamb—and that when it's a shilling a pound—as late as ten o'clock, to be cooked that night for supper. They like their nick-nacks too, and often my boy is running all over the town to get them sweetbreads for breakfast.' 'You'd think, to stand a-top of the street and take a view of it both sides of the way, right to the bottom, that they wouldn't trouble me much except it was for butter-scrapings and bacon hocks and that sort of thing,' said the cheesemonger; 'Lor' bless you! It ain't single, no, nor yet double Glo'ster that'll do for 'em. It must be best Cheshire or none. Same with butter. Same with ham and eggs. The very best and never mind the price is their motto.' The ruffians of Keate Street, however, are not all of this superior order. The common pickpocket finds a home there, and the 'smasher,' and the area sneak, and the 'snow gatherer,' as the rascal who makes the thieving of linen his special study poetically styles himself; and, worse than all, a swarm of likely young fellows who as yet cannot lay claim to be called robbers, but who are satisfactorily progressing under the teaching of Moss Jacobs and Barney Davis. If roguery stands there would be no approaching Little Keate Street by a mile.

I should not like to say that Hatton Wall was, in a Keate Street sense, as ugly as Keate Street. I have not such great enmity against the organ grinders as to wish that it might be. To look at, however, it is uglier: a horribly dark, dingy, antiquated place, all gutter and cobble-stones, and smelling as strong of Irish as Neal's Buildings itself. The police, as we observed, went in pairs; and when *this* is the case in a neighbourhood, you may mark it as one in which it would be unsafe to openly consult your gold lever in order to ascertain the time. I ventured the insinuation that perhaps we had better retrace our steps, and come again some other night—some moonlight night, but our artist, who is as brave as he is big, at once taunted me with cowardice, and declared that since I had drawn him into the mess he would see the end of it, even though he searched every nook and alley in the place; and immediately proceeded to carry out his valiant determination by inquiring of a little boy, that moment emerging from a scowling little public-house near Bleeding Hart Yard, hugging a gin bottle, whether he would be so obliging as to inform us where the organ men were to be found.

The little fellow replied that he was jiggered if he knew;—that they lived a'most anywhere about there, 'down here, mostly, and over there; and a good many up that there way, if you means their lodgings;' and he indicated 'down here' and 'over there' by pointing with his gin-bottle, and in the same manner gave us to understand which was 'that there way,' which was not at all an inviting way, being more dismal than any we had yet traversed, narrow, miry, and flanked on either side by little-windowed houses, tall, dingy, and mysterious-looking enough to be haunted—or at least in Chancery. However, it was the organ man's 'lodgings' that we did mean, and so we manfully struck into the unclean crevice, known as Little Saffron Hill.

But though we perambulated the dingy thoroughfare in the most careful manner, no organ man could we find either entering or emerging from his domicile. Once my companion thought that he descried the object of our pursuit ascending the steps of a distant house, and with a subdued exclamation of triumph he started off to see; in a few seconds, however, he returned disconsolate to report the mistaken figure a woman with a clothes-basket. At that instant, however, and while we were at a standstill, the lively notes of a polka suddenly greeted our ears, and eagerly following the welcome sound, we presently arrived at the house from whence it proceeded. It was a private house, quite an ordinary-looking habitation, with the same closed shutters and dingy door as the rest, and no more than the average amount of light glimmering through the chinks, to bespeak it a place of amusement. Still, however, as we stood and listened on the steps of the house, we were convinced that it must be. The polka ceased, and was instantly followed by a jig in the same lively measure; moreover there was the hum of many voices, and the sounds of the shuffling of feet.

'It is a threepenny hop,—there can't be a doubt of it,' said we; and feeling in our pocket for the necessary entrance-money, we boldly pushed open the door and entered.

The passage was dark, but at the end of it there was a door of a room, in which there was evidently plenty of light, and in which, as we could now plainly make out, the music and dancing was. Without a moment's hesitation we stepped up to this door, as to the first, and pushed it open.

Our expectations, however, were not exactly realized. In an instant we found ourselves, not in a dancing-room but in a workshop—an establishment for the manufacture and repair of street organs. It was a small place, no bigger, probably, than an ordinary dining-room, but it was chokeful of organs, old and new,—stacked against the walls, on the floor, and on work-benches. Eight or ten bare-armed, bearded Italians were busy, patching, and polishing, and tinkering at the instruments. The jig tune that had attracted us was still proceeding as we entered, the organ from which it was produced standing on the ground, and the performer kneeling before it gravely grinding at the handle. It was the property, as it seemed, of an unmistakeable street grinder, who stood by, watching the music doctor as he examined the ailing organ, with as anxious and distressed a countenance as though it were nothing less precious than his eldest born brought to be tested on account of some suspected intestinal disorder.

Patchers, polishers, tinkers—even the man that was grinding the jig—paused in their various occupations and regarded us inquiringly. The situation was embarrassing, the more so that the door had slammed to, and we were shut in, and we laboured under the disadvantage of not knowing a word of the Italian tongue.

'Vat you bisniss?' demanded the street grinder, presuming on his knowledge of our language to be spokesman.

We had no business—none, at least, that could be explained in an off-hand and satisfactory manner. My companion attempted the explanation, however.

'It's all right,' said he, with an insinuating little laugh—'it's a little mistake — we thought there was something going on—don't mind us.'

The organ grinder merely replied, 'Aha!' as far as we could make out; but, turning to the workmen, the traitorous villain must have altogether misinterpreted to them my companion's observation, for they rose, with warlike gestures and ejaculations, and turned as one man against us,—luckily, however, with so much noise that the proprietor of the premises, who was engaged in an adjoining apartment, was disturbed, and came hurriedly in to see what the row was about. He was a civil fellow, and listened with polite attention to what we had to say. His knowledge of English, however, could scarcely have been so 'perfect' as, at starting, he assured us it was; that is, judging from his answers.

'Oh yes! what you say is exact, gentlemen; but you cannot dance here for threepence or for any money. If you will dance, you must go to Badessa, or to Sugar Loaf, or to Golden Anchor. Good evening, gentlemen.' And he showed us to the door.

Although this little adventure could not be said to be in all respects gratifying, it was so in the main, inasmuch as it provided us with a clue. Clearly the places enumerated by the worthy organ builder were places of public entertainment—places where dancing was encouraged. Where was the Golden Anchor? Opportunely there came by a policeman.

'Keep straight on and cross the road, and it's the second public on the left.'

'It is a place where organ men assemble for their amusement, is it not?'

'You'll precious soon find the sort of place it is before you get within a dozen yards of it,' replied the policeman. And so directed we once more stepped out through the mire and the drizzling rain, with hope revived.

Since we paid a visit to the Golden Anchor, that hostel has earned for itself a hideous notoriety. Murder has been done there. At least that is how the law, misled by police pig-headedness and the reckless oath-taking of false witnesses, at first called it; but now, as it appears, the result of the bloody broil there enacted was merely a man slaughtered and not murdered—one man slaughtered and two or three others maimed and gashed and prodded! It was a pity that the disgraceful bungle was not completed by the hanging of an innocent man before Newgate. The Golden Anchor would have 'drawn' then with a vengeance, and done such a trade as never was the like; as it is the enterprising and conscientious landlord reaps little or no advantage from the perpetration in his house of the pretty little tragedy.

At the time we were in search of it, however, it had no special attraction; and it was not without some little difficulty that we discovered it —a low, broad house, gay with gas, clean looking, and standing at the corner of a lane leading to that dismal waste opposite the railway station in New Victoria Street, patronized by that miserable dreg of humanity, the betting blackguard. In the distance the house looked so quiet and decent that, despite the emblem of hope blazoned in gold above the doorway, we should have thought ourselves again at fault had it not been for the tokens the policeman had hinted at, and which were made known to us, not at one dozen yards' distance off, but at three at the very least.

It was not a sound of mirth, neither could it be mistaken for quarreling. It was an uproar composed of single ejaculations, delivered by many voices, and with a vehemence that was absolutely startling. It was as though a multitude of strong-lunged religious fanatics had seized on a victim and were, in set form, cursing him, dwelling with demoniac relish on each syllable of the anathema, by way of transfixing the soul of the poor wretch with horror. At the same time there smote on the listening ear a hollow thumping noise that would well have passed as the rapping of poignard handles on the lid of an empty coffin.

Nor did a glimpse of the interior of the mysterious caravanserai, afforded by the swinging ajar of its centre door, do much toward dispelling the suspicion that some mystic and terrible ceremony was in progress within. There was to be seen a ferocious band seated about a long table, while one stood up in their midst, in a fiercely excited attitude, and continually raising both his clenched fists above his head, and bringing them down on to the table with a bang. And yet, marvel of marvels! the individual that opened the door was a little girl with a beer jug in her hand, and she went elbowing close by the fierce denouncer, with no more apparent concern than though he had been a peep-show man describing the wonders of his theatre. Surely where so helpless a creature went we might venture,—so in we went.

A glance explained the mystery. The bar was very long, and the space before it ample. There were butts and tables and forms in this space; and about the tables and the butts were grouped knots of Italians, young and old, playing at their national game of *moro*—a simple game enough, as the reader is perhaps aware; a sort of combination of the English boys' games of 'buck buck' and 'odds and evens,' tho seated players watching the upraised hands of 'buck,' and in their turn anticipating the number of fingers 'buck' intends displaying by the time his rapidly descending fists reach the table-top. In the hands of these Italians, however, it was a terrible game. With flashing eye and dishevelled hair, the callers, too eager to keep their seats, half rose and leant over the table, roaring out their guesses, with their noses nearly touching that of 'buck,' —the deep chest voices of the men, the high-pitched clamour of the lads, the laughter of the lucky guessers, and the disappointed growls of the unlucky ones, blending to make a scene most bedlamitish. It seemed a conflict for blood rather than for beer. Nevertheless, they were a jolly, good-tempered crew enough; and as the games came to an end (there were at least half a dozen games in progress at the various tables), they came jovially to the bar and drank their liquor, with much joking and friendly shoulder-slapping. They paid down their losings, too, with the air of fellows who had spare sixpences to spend; indeed, they seemed to be so flush of money that we began to doubt if they could possibly be men who mucked up a day's earnings a halfpenny at a time by grinding at an organ, and took opportunity to ask the waiter (the poor wretch, probably, who afterwards was so nearly fatally-tabbed in the stomach) if such were the case.

'They ain't all organ men,' he replied; 'some of 'em are picture-frame makers, and image-coves. They are about half organ men.'

'They seem to spend their money pretty freely.'

'So they ought; they earns enough.'

'What, the organ men?'

'Organ men, ah! A'pence tells up, don't yer know. They picks up a jolly sight more than me and you, as works hard for our livin'.'

There was nothing in the dress of the *moro* players to distinguish the organ grinder from his friend the 'image cove.' All were dressed alike—and very well dressed, after a style. More than anything they looked like a body of seafaring men — foreign sailors, recently paid off. Their long blue jackets were those of holiday-dressed sailors, as were their black satin waistcoats, their 'navy' caps, their pumps and their earrings, and their abundance of silver watch-guard. Moreover, most of them wore bright-coloured worsted comforters, as do foreign sailors invariably when dressed in their best and ashore. Altogether, their appearance was such as to entirely change one's views concerning the beggarly trade of organ grinding.

Meanwhile our friends carouse, and the moro players cluster thicker about the tables and butts, and the din becomes such that the tall and muscular landlord has to hold his hand to his ear that he may catch the orders of his customers. Suddenly, however, a sound of music is heard, and instantly there is a commotion amongst the players, and all but those who are in the middle of a game hurry towards a door at the end of a passage beside the bar. Joining the throng, we too approach the door and enter the room it opens into.

It is that to which the organ builder recommended us, 'if we must dance.' It is a spacious room, with bare, dirty walls, and scant of furniture as the casual ward of a workhouse. There is only one large table in the place, and a-top of that is mounted a hard-working grinder, in his every-day clothes, with his organ at his side, and labouring at the handle of it as stolidly, and with the same business air as though he were standing in the gutter in the Edgware Road. Amongst the throng that crowd the room he must recognize many friends—relatives, perhaps,—but he looks as unconcerned as a soldier on duty in a barrack-yard. Perhaps he would not get so many halfpence if he affected to regard his services as merely friendly

As it is he does not fare badly. Between each polka and waltz he makes a significant pause, and the dancers fee him. There are female dancers as well as male; and, strangely enough, the females are not one of them Italian. They are chiefly English and Irish girls, working in the neighbourhood as looking-glass frame polishers We were informed by one of the damsels in question that the Italians *never* bring their countrywomen with them to the dancing-room. Perhaps this may be accounted for on economical grounds; did they bring their countrywomen with them, they would naturally expect to be treated with some degree of generosity; whereas the grinder's treatment of his English or Irish partner was as shabby as can be well imagined, her only reward being a pull at the pewter pot out of which he himself regaled. True, he did not ask much of her; indeed, his contract with her could scarcely be said to amount to a partnership, the dance being managed in this strange fashion:—Jacko and Antonio make up their minds for a dance, and select each a damsel; but Jacko and Antonio dance together, and the two damsels dance together alongside Jacko and friend. When the dance is over, Jacko orders four pen'north of beer, and the four divide it amongst them.

'Stingy beggars, arn't they?' whispered the damsel who had given us the bit of information concerning the organ man's peculiar method of dancing; 'thinks as much of a shilling as another man would of five. It ain't as though it was every night.'

'They don't come here every night in the week?'

'Bless you, no! a few on Mondays, sometimes, but nothing to speak of. Saturday night is their time—their time out, I mean: Sunday is their time at home.'

'Their time for what?—not dancing?'

'Dancing, no! no room for dancing, with twelve or fourteen of 'em in a bit of a back parlour. Drinking and cards and dominoes, that's what they get up to. Let 'em alone; they can come out strong enough amongst their own set. Plenty to eat and drink, plenty of rum, plenty of everything.'

'I shouldn't have thought that they earned sufficient money to indulge in such luxuries.'

'They don't earn it all: see what their wives earn at artificial-flower making and cigar-making.'

'Then they have pretty comfortable homes?'

'Well, comfortable as they look at it: you see, they are people of such strange ways: all for "clubbing." They club together to pay the rent of a room; to buy a joint of meat; for their beer, for their tobacco, for everything; eating and drinking and smoking together, a whole houseful of 'em, just as though they were all brothers and sisters. Plenty of everything, you know, but such a hugger-mugger.'

The young woman spoke as one that knew; and it was very much to our annoyance that, just at this moment, Jacko once more advanced towards her, and invited her to stand up and earn another drink of bad beer; and so we lost sight of her.

We had gleaned enough, one way and another, however, to convince us that Jacko makes a very decent livelihood out of his organ. He lives well, takes his amusement, has a bettermost suit of clothes, and a silver watch and chain.

'Which is crowning evidence,' triumphantly observes the grinder's champion, 'that the public are well disposed towards the poor fellow, that they appreciate his humble efforts to amuse them, and properly reward him.'

But isn't there another point of observation from which the flourishing grinder may be viewed? We humbly and hopefully think so. Assuming—and surely it is fair to assume—that at least half the grinder's gleanings accrue to him as 'smart money' to send him and his nuisance packing, our eyes are opened to the immense strength of this section of the army of opposition—a section more powerful than any other, and one that has only to vigorously assert itself, and the days of the organ monster's reign are numbered.

JAMES GREENWOOD.

MODERN BEAU BRUMMELLISM.

BEAU BRUMMELL was the dandy of his day, and a dandy of a peculiar kind. Etymologists tell us that the word 'dandy' is derived from the French *dandin*, or 'ninny,' or from the Italian *dandola*, or 'toy.' Hence a dandy means one who dresses himself like a doll, a fop, a coxcomb, a ninny. The peculiar type which was especially represented by the famous Brummell was combined with an amount of fastidiousness and helplessness to which there is no parallel. He was a remarkable instance of a man pushing himself into a grade of society to which he had no claim, by dint of a certain amount of assurance and a high estimation of himself. There is nothing more true than the saying that the world takes a man at the value he sets upon himself. He who depreciates himself by a humility, whether true or false, will not be esteemed by the world at large. The dealer who cries 'stinking fish' is not likely to find much custom for his wares. Let a man assert himself, and lay claim to a certain amount of wisdom, and talk like an oracle, and the chances are that, unless he is a fool, the world, having neither time nor inclination to go into the matter, will take him at his own valuation. It only requires perseverance, an indomitable will, and inordinate self esteem, combined with a certain amount of tact, which, in this instance, might almost be better called an instinct of self-preservation, which prevents a man from showing the cards which he holds in his own hands. Some people are easily imposed upon by silence, and are apt to attribute depth of learning and profundity of thought to the man who is silent, for no other reason than that he has nothing to say. Coleridge says, 'Silence does not always mark wisdom;' and goes on to relate an anecdote in illustration. 'I was at dinner, some time ago, in company with a man who listened to me and said nothing for a long time; but he nodded his head, and I thought him intelligent. At length, towards the end of dinner, some apple dumplings were placed on the table, and my man had no sooner seen them than he burst forth with "Them's the jockeys for me!" He destroyed whatever *prestige* he had acquired by his silence by showing his folly.' Had he remained silent, Coleridge might have continued to think him intelligent. The man who is wise enough to keep his own counsel while he lays claim to superior gifts, will probably get credit for all he claims. In Brummell we have a remarkable instance of a man valued according to his own estimate of himself. Possessing no great mental gifts, he worked his way into the highest ranks of society, until he came into the very presence of royalty, where he made himself necessary by the force of will, assurance, and self-conceit, which had already obtained for him so great a reputation, that to be spoken to by Brummell, and to dress like him, was the ambition of all the dandies of the day. No doubt he possessed great graces of the body, as well as the natural gift of an almost faultless taste: otherwise it would be impossible fully to account for the completeness of his success while he basked in the sunshine of royal favour. He was the very type of dandies,

'neat, trimly dress'd,
Fresh as a bridegroom . . .
* * *
He was perfumed like a milliner,
And 'twixt his finger and his thumb he held
A pouncet-box, which ever and anon
He gave his nose, and took 't away again.'

Stories without end are told of him, all pointing to him as the great oracle in dress. No lady ever required the attention of her handmaid more than Brummell demanded the assistance of his valet during the tedious operation of his toilet. The great secret of tying a cravat was known only to Brummell and his set; and it is reported of him that his servant was seen to leave his presence with a large quantity of tumbled cravats, which, on being interrogated, he said were 'failures,' so important were cravats in those days, and so critical the tying of them. His fastidiousness and helplessness are exhibited side by side in this anecdote. The one that there should have been so many 'failures' before he could be satisfied; the other, that he should have required the assistance of a valet, or, indeed, of any hand except his own in tying it.

This fastidiousness and helplessness are not, however, confined to any age. Indolence, conceit, love of dress, and helplessness, will always exist so long as we have bodies to pamper and to deck. There will always be men who devote much time and thought to their personal appearance, who 'shine so brisk, and smell so sweet, and talk so like a waiting gentlewoman;' men who try on coat after coat, and waistcoat after waistcoat, that their effect may be faultless; who consider harmony of colour, and the cut of a coat, or the fit of a shoe, or a boot, matters of the greatest moment in life; who, whether beardless boys or elderly men, never pass a looking-glass without stealing sly glances at themselves, and never move except with care and caution, lest the arrangement of their hair, or some portion of their toilet, should be marred. The elderly dandies study to be *bien conservés*, while the younger ones care only never to be behind the fashion of the day, be it what it may. In a certain listlessness of manner they, like Brummell, demand the constant attention of a valet. They require him to stand behind them and arrange the parting of their hair at the back of the head and to smoothe it, to make the collar and tie tie well, to tighten the waistcoat, and put on the coat artistically, and press out any creases; to put the right quantity of perfume on the hankerchief, and, in fine, to be responsible for their appearance. These dandies cannot lace or unlace their own boots; they cannot take off their own coat; and never for a moment dream of packing their own clothes, or of looking after their own luggage when they travel. They look for, expect, and demand an amount of attention which any, who do not happen to be somewhat behind the scenes, would suppose none but the most helpless of women would require. It by no means follows that they have been brought up in such Sybarite habits. Love of ease, love of self-importance, or a mistaken idea that it indicates high breeding, have led to this unmanliness. There is no greater mistake than to suppose that they who have been most accustomed to what are called the luxuries of life from their very cradle are the most dependent upon them. Perhaps some of the most independent men are to be found among those who have all their lives been in the full enjoyment of every comfort, while, on the other hand, they who have come into possession of them only recently, and by a lucky stroke of fortune, lay the most stress upon them, and are very tenacious of them, as if the secret of true happiness were bound up in them. Nothing illustrates this more than the noble and manly way in which some of those who had been brought up in the very lap of luxury bore the hardships and adversities of a soldier's life during the war in the Crimea. Then it was that the true metal showed itself; that good blood proved itself by noble deeds.

It cannot be denied that it would be difficult to devise anything more hideous or unbecoming than the dress of a gentleman of the nineteenth century. It may be easy and comfortable, and a wider margin may be allowed to the caprice of individuals; but, in all its forms, it is ugly and deficient in both picturesque and pictorial effect. One of the great charms of Vandyke's pictures, apart, of course, from their exquisite painting, lies in the dress. They are all such courtly gentlemen, and one feels to be in such good company as one admires them. Theirs was no fancy dress put on for the occasion, no special dandyism, but the ordinary dress of the times, such as men of their rank and position were accustomed to wear. There was much more etiquette in dress formerly than now exists, just as there was much more formality in all they did. Ruffles and buckles, silk hose and doublets, were not adopted specially by any one more devoted than his neighbours to the love and science of dress. Men and women were more courteous to one another, outwardly at least, than they now are. Children rose up at the entrance of their parents, and did not resume their seats while they were standing. No man would address any lady in public with his head covered. Young men would take off their hats even to their equals, always to their elders. The old *minuet de la cour* was a very sedate kind of dance compared with those of the present day. If we have gained in freedom, we have lost a great deal of outward mutual respect. Much of what we mean still remains on the Continent, where there is a considerable distinction between the various classes in matters of dress. The peasant has his or her style, and the nobles theirs, while the intermediate classes have their distinctive styles. These distinctions are now abolished. We have no national costume; and the lowest menials endeavour to imitate, to the best of their powers, the grandest lords and ladies in the land.

It would be a great mistake to infer, from the pictures which have been handed down to us, that there was more dandyism formerly than now. Who would lay anything of the kind to the charge of Lord Nelson? Yet we find him represented to us, in paintings descriptive of his great naval actions, dressed in knee-breeches, silk stockings, and all the accessories of a court dress.

It was the custom which prevailed at that period, and is by no means a fashion in the sense in which the word is used to denote super-excellence and super-fastidiousness in dress. At the death of Lord Nelson the officers who surrounded that great hero are depicted dressed according to the custom which was as much *de rigueur* as it is now for officers in the army and navy to put on their uniforms when they go into the presence of royalty. To compare small things with great, we find that Lord Winchilsea's Eleven played at cricket in silver-laced hats, knee-breeches, and silk stockings. Bumps and even blood would occasionally show and come through the stockings; and it is related of one man that he tore a finger-nail off against his shoe-buckle in picking up a ball! There must have been a very different kind of bowling then to that which now prevails, if we may judge from the necessity for pads of all kinds and descriptions, and when, in spite of pads and gloves, fingers and, occasionally, even legs are broken by the excessive violence of the bowling.

The formality and courtliness in dress which existed even to so late a period as that to which we have referred, may be said to have gone out with hoops and powder. Our ancestors, no doubt, deplored the changes which took place in their days, and sighed over the introduction of novelties, and the freedom or license, as it may be called, in dress in our times would have shocked their sense of propriety, for we find an amusing account in the 'Spectator' of the alarm felt at the way in which ladies dressed themselves for riding, 'in a hat and feather, a riding-coat and periwig, or at least tying up their hair in a bag or riband, in imitation of the smart part of the opposite sex,' which the astonished countryman described as 'a gentleman in a coat and hat.'

There can be no doubt that a certain amount of attention to dress is necessary so far as it effects personal cleanliness and neatness. A well-dressed man, that is to say, a man who dresses like a gentleman, neither like a fop, nor a clerk, nor a tailor who makes his own back his advertisement, is sure to be well received in all good society. Goldsmith says that 'Processions, cavalcades, and all that fund of gay frippery furnished out by tailors, barbers, and tirewomen, mechanically influence the mind into veneration; an emperor in his nightcap would not meet with half the respect of an emperor with a crown.' The only complaint made against our gracious Queen, when she visited Ireland, by some of her poor Irish subjects was, that 'she was dressed like any other lady, and had no crown on her head.' There is much worldly wisdom in paying some heed to the adornment of the outer man. It is a good letter of introduction; but when it goes beyond that, and branches out into excesses of foppery, it becomes unmanly, and, as such, cannot be too much condemned. When young men are either so helpless or fastidious that the constant presence of a valet during their toilet is a *sine quâ non*; that the parting at the back of the head requires as much attention as a lady's 'back hair;' it is time, indeed, that some such satirist as the old 'Spectator' should rise up and turn them into ridicule.

But of all the fops in existence, the old fop is the most contemptible. A man who has outlived his generation; who trips like Agag 'delicately,' to hide the infirmities of age, or affect a youth that has long ceased; who competes with the young men of the day in his attentions to the fair sex; who dresses in the very extreme of the prevailing fashion of the day, with shirts elaborately embroidered, and wristbands, fastened together with conspicuously magnificent sleeve-links, which he is always pulling down, either to show them or to establish the fact, which no one would care to dispute, that he has a clean shirt to his back; who is scented and perfumed; whose wig, faultlessly made, is judiciously sprinkled with a few grey hairs that it may appear to be his own hair when he has long ceased to have any to boast of; who uses dyes and cosmetics that the marks of age may be obliterated and the bloom of youth imitated; who is in a flutter of delight when any one conversant with his weakness is kind enough to mistake him for his own son or the husband of one of his daughters; such a man is an object of both pity and contempt. When age is not accompanied by wisdom, but exhibits only the folly of which man's weakness is capable, it is a hopeless case.

Dirty fops are an especial abomination. Men, young or old, who are at great pains to adorn themselves without the most scrupulous regard to cleanliness; who wear many rings upon very indifferently washed fingers; who hang themselves in chains of gold; whose shirt fronts present the greatest variety, at different times, of the most costly jewellery; whose discoloured teeth and ill-brushed hair are a revelation in themselves,— such men only make their defect the more conspicuous by the decorations with which they overlay it. It is related of a *grande dame* who was remarkable for her wit and beauty, that she rejected a man of considerable note in the world, as well as an 'exquisite,' of his day, and who was one of her most devoted admirers, for no other reason than that she saw ensconced between his teeth, when he made his appearance at breakfast, a piece of spinach which she had noticed the evening before. It is impossible for any one, whether man, woman, or child, to be too particular about cleanliness of person and of habits. In these days, when there are such facilities for washing, and when all appliances are so easy of attainment, it is perfectly inexcusable in any one to fail in cleanliness; and of all people, the fop, who professes to make his person his study, is the most inexcusable if he neglect the fundamental principle of dandyism, which is, in fact, its chief, if not its only recommendation.

It has been said that the youth who is not more or less a dandy, will grow into an untidy, slovenly man. There may be some truth in this. Indeed, we should be sorry to see any young man altogether indifferent about his personal appearance. It is not that which offends. It is rather the excess to which it is carried; when self becomes the all-absorbing subject upon which thought, time, and labour are spent; when it degenerates into foppery, into an effeminacy, into a certain listlessness, helplessness, and affectation which are unworthy of a man. It is finicalness of dandyism, and not its neatness and cleanliness, that we quarrel with, on the principle that whatever detracts from manliness is unworthy of a man.

THE 'BEAUX MONDES' OF PARIS AND LONDON.

IT is now some months since one of the leading and most popular journals of the day directed the public attention to a very remarkable phase of society in Paris. It seems that a certain portion of the *beau monde* of that capital, impelled by an incredible impulse (whether for good or evil who can tell?), made advances to the *demi monde*, and both sought and obtained admission within the precincts of that society. It almost surpasses belief, that women of fair reputation, of good descent, and of high repute in the best Parisian society should, for the sake of an idle curiosity, condescend to desire an acquaintance with the life, manners, and customs, of a certain class of women whose position and circumstances denote the very reverse of purity and chastity, and who keep a kind of court which is attended by all the men of wealth and fashion between twenty and sixty. It is possible that the *beau monde* may have desired to solve the problem why there existed so great a disinclination for matrimony, and what those charms were which attracted so many from their homes and made them truants. They may have wished to reclaim some who had wandered from their allegiance, but it was a rash experiment and one which nothing could justify. Their presence sanctioned that against which their whole life was, or ought to have been, a protest. They descended from their high position, and if they have sullied their own reputation they have no one to blame but themselves. If mere idle curiosity was their motive they were, of course, still more without excuse. We all know how fatal a gift curiosity is, and how much woe it has worked. Our common mother Eve was not proof against it, and we are sufferers. How could they hope to escape its penalties if they were bent upon indulging it at all risks? But there is a much graver question underlying this peculiar phase of Parisian society. Is it that in France there is a different code of morals to that which prevails wherever Christianity is taught? Is it that French morality and French decency are names without a meaning, and that Paris is more honeycombed with vice than any other city? Is it that the Court is less pure or the general tone of society more corrupt? Is it that home influences are unknown or depreciated? It is a remarkable fact, when taken in combination with the flourishing condition of the *demi monde* and the recognized 'status' it has in Paris, that a French family is proverbially small; so much so that the contrary is looked upon as quite exceptional, which a French lady of our acquaintance spoke of as being *comme les Anglais*.

It was not long after our attention had been drawn to the existing state of things, that we read an acount of the magnificence of a house in Paris belonging to a lady whose ambition it was to eclipse all her rivals in *luxe*. In addition to the boundless expenditure which she lavished upon it, she ordered, it was said, four pictures of herself to be painted after a peculiar fashion, which shall be nameless. In one of them, which has been completed, she is represented as Cleopatra, as she rises up in her unveiled beauty before the 'dull, cold-blooded Cæsar,' into whose presence she had been introduced within the folds of a carpet. This speaks volumes, and needs no comment. If such *lionnes* are the rage of the fashionable and artistic world of Paris, we cannot be surprised that there should be any approximation to an *entente cordiale* between the *beau monde* and the *demi monde*. We remember to have heard some years ago an Englishman, who had married a foreigner, declare that he would never allow his wife to have a French woman for her friend, as he believed there was scarcely one good one amongst them. This was a sweeping condemnation against which we were not slow to protest, because we have ourselves known several who are examples of all that is good and pure. But after the revelations that have lately been made, we are inclined to fear that general society is not conspicuous for its morality.

Paris has reached a climax in what is generally called civilization that cannot be surpassed. She has adorned and beautified herself with a rapidity and splendour that are without a parallel. She is the most beautiful capital in the world—the queen of cities; she has put out of sight all that can offend the taste of the most refined critics; she has driven further and further back all the signs of poverty and labour which might offend the eye or suggest a thought inconsistent with the opulence and gaiety with which it is her desire to impress her visitors; she is a very Sybarite of cities; but with all her magnificence of decoration, with all her lavish outlay and ever-changing caprice, which constitutes her the leader of fashion throughout Europe, she carries within herself the elements of her own ruin, which cannot be far distant. No society can last long which is so rotten at its core, where profligacy reigns, and all sense of propriety is at a discount.

The history of the world supplies abundant instances of cities which have reached a climax of refined splendour, and, being lifted up in their pride, have overlooked virtue, and have been dashed to the ground, and have crumbled to ruin; nor need France go far to look for such an example. In the period before the great French Revolution society had become corrupt. They who ought to have been examples of virtue made use of their high and exalted position for the indulgence of their evil passions, and saw in it only opportunities for a vicious life. Even now men tremble at the recollection of the awful judgment that fell upon them, which has left that fair and beautiful country in a state of ferment from which there seems to be no repose, and which can only be kept under by the firm hand of a great military power which is ever ready to repress the first indication of the popular mind daring to think for itself.

We have said that there is a deeper and graver question underlying the present aspect of society in Paris. May it not be that there is throughout society, in every part of the world, a general uprising against restrictions of all kinds? Freedom and liberty are the watchwords of all parties and all nations, and the separation between them and licentiousness and license is very narrow and quickly got over. Under their high-sounding names much wrong is done; spoliation and lawlessness shelter themselves there, and every one claims for himself the right to do what seems to him good in his own eyes. It is impossible to help seeing that there is a growing dislike to all authority, to everything which imposes a fetter upon the human will. Children are quick to throw off the restraints of parental authority; married people to live more separate lives; scholars to sit in judgment on their teachers; congregations to dismiss their preachers; the clergy to set at nought their bishops; politicians to foment discord and rebellion when it suits their purpose to do so. The disposition to reduce the law of both church and state down to the very minimum of its letter is one of the prevailing faults of the age. The first promptings of the human intellect of the present day is to dispute, step by step, every demand which is made upon it in the name of authority; and we believe it to be this temper which tends to the severance of those ties, and the depreciation of those maxims which are the bond and safeguard of society.

There are certain usages and customs better known by the somewhat indefinite term of the *convenances* of society, which have become to some extent law, and have a prescriptive right to our respectful attention and consideration. Against these the mind of the nineteenth century rebels. Old customs and traditions are treated with the utmost contempt and set at nought, and in the manners of the rising generation there is expressed the most decided resistance to that delicacy of thought and consideration for others which formerly served to make men keep out of sight any infringement against good morals. It may be said that the motive was low—that it was a mere feeling of human respect, and, as such, of but little value; yet, even if so, it surely had the advantage over that most culpable disregard for appearances which leads to the public exhibition of vice. In the fact that men dare not associate publicly with vicious companions there lies a protest on the part of society in general against their evil doings; but the moment they cease to restrain their conduct within due limits, and unblushingly pursue their course, and society still tolerates them and winks at their effrontery, there is no longer any safeguard against its utter demoralization.

We owe a vast debt to those who have raised their voices in condemnation of the attitude of the *beau monde* towards the *demi monde* of Paris. We do not entertain the opinion held by some that it is better not to speak of these things, but simply to ignore them as if they did not exist; for if we have a serious malady, or a wound in any part of our bodies, we do not gain anything by pretending that we have it not; and we hold that it is, to say the least, unwise to shut our eyes to the fact that a revolution of an important character has taken place in society.

In public matters there is nothing wrong in pointing out a scandal where it exists. To ferret out a neighbour's faults, and to expose them to the public gaze, is an infringement of the law of charity. But that which is a blot in the intercourse of individuals with each other, chameleon-like, changes its hue altogether when it becomes a question of nation against nation. National customs, national tastes, national faults, are a safe mark for other nations to hit at pleasure. In the first place, what is national is more or less public property—there is no exposure of 'secret faults;' and, in the second place, the principle of self-protection justifies it, because we may avert evil from ourselves by noting its existence and its ruinous consequences elsewhere. We may effect a kind of moral quarantine by which dangerous and polluting influences shall be kept at a distance. It becomes a duty to note and comment upon the signs of the times, and to take warning from every false step which others make. We may thereby arrest the progress of evil at home, and expose the snares and pitfalls which lie concealed beneath a specious exterior; only let us be sure of one thing— that we are equally clearsighted as to our own defects.

'O wad some Power the giftie gie us
To see oursels as others see us,
It wad frae mony a blunder free us,
And foolish notion.'

There is no fault into which we are more apt to fall than that of being keen to detect errors and shortcomings in others, and slow in discovering our own. As individuals we have no right to do so. But the law which is intended to seal the lips of those who are addicted to evil speaking has no such restrictive power where nations and the public good are concerned. It is said that, as a rule, no class of persons is so censorious as the highly moral. There is something, perhaps, in the unassailableness of virtue and morality which tempts the virtuous to throw stones; and we are disposed to think that it is the tendency of all nations, but especially of Englishmen, to hold the customs, traditions, and manners of all other countries cheap.

It is a matter of fact that, with all our national pride, we are, in many instances, the most servile copyists of the French, and it will be well for us to inquire whether the spirit of this century has not led us in the same direction as that which we so justly condemn in our neighbours. Are there any indications of a similar movement on this side of the Channel? Can we detect any signs and sounds of its advent among us? There is no wisdom in throwing dust in our own eyes; to be forewarned is to be forearmed, and we are inclined to think that there are sufficient grounds for apprehension.

Not many years ago it would

have been considered to be the very acme of indecency and impudence for any of the thoughtless young men who abound, more or less, in every capital to recognize, or to appear even to notice in public, any of those fair 'unfortunates' who lie in wait 'to hunt souls.' They would have been distressed beyond measure at the idea that their mothers or sisters should suspect, much more know, of their having formed any *liaison* so dangerous and disreputable. But such tenderness of conscience, such regard for the proprieties of life, scarcely remains. It is no uncommon thing for a young man to appear in the Park escorting a 'celebrity' of this kind, and, as he passes some lady of his acquaintance, to lift his hat in courteous recognition of her, as though there were nothing to be ashamed of in his companion. Nor is it rare for a popular character to appear at the Opera, exquisitely dressed, and with some pretence of modesty in her attire, in one of the most conspicuous boxes, surrounded by her admirers, whose relations witness their infatuation from the opposite tier. Nor is this all. The very names of these women have become so notorious that they are in the mouths of many of the fast young ladies of our *beau monde*. How they have come to such a knowledge let others tell; but they speak of them, of their 'turn out,' and their horsemanship, and note their dress and style, and can tell the 'Skittles' ponies at a distance, and the precise hour at which she drives into the Park; how she wears her hat, the colour of her horse and habit, and even go so far as to dress after her, taking their cue from her as if they envied her her power of attraction. It is notorious that many of the changes which we have witnessed of late years in hats and petticoats have originated from celebrities of this kind, and we fear it is an indication of a disposition on the part of our *beau monde* to take a leaf out of the book of the *beau monde* of Paris. There was also a symptom of a like tendency in the strange freak which so engrossed all our fine ladies a few years ago when nothing would satisfy them but 'a night at Cremorne.' They were possessed by a strange and most ill-advised curiosity to know something of its attractions, and to acquaint themselves with one of the popular haunts of the *demi monde*. It is true that our noble countrywomen shut out for the time its usual patronesses, and monopolized it to themselves, and that in this respect they did not go so deep into the mire as our foreign neighbours would have done, who would have preferred it un-Romfordized; but in other respects it exhibits the same tendency to overstep the barrier between them and their frail sisterhood, which we would earnestly implore them never to lower for any consideration. We think that, taking all things into account, the disposition which exists to trample out of sight all the finer lines which until lately regulated the social intercourse of the upper classes, and the very great license which is given to the tongue, by which the fine edge of modesty is blunted, we shall do well to look at home before we are so loud in our condemnation of others. Burns's lines to the 'unco' guid' are never out of season—

'A' ye wha are sae guid yoursel,
  Sae pious and sae holy;
Ye've nocht to do but mark and tell
  Your neebours' faults and folly.'

If we have as yet escaped the contamination which must, we fear, precede such an act as that by which the *beau monde* of Paris degraded itself, it is still an undoubted fact that we are not standing on such a pinnacle of superior sanctity and morality that we can reasonably congratulate ourselves that we are 'not as other men.'

BALLS IN VIENNA.

A FEW years ago and no European capital was less visited by our countrymen and countrywomen than Vienna. In the days of Metternich despotisms, *malice prepense* aggravated the inevitable pains of locomotion with a machinery well calculated to keep the Austrian frontiers clear of mere holiday travellers. So that in the days of passports and police, few strangers came to the Imperial city except on business. Vienna contained, it is true, a colony of respectable English, who had settled on the banks of the Danube for purposes of economy or pleasure. But since paper money has driven away the metallic coinage, low prices have taken to themselves wings, so that Vienna is at present the dearest of European cities, except St. Petersburg, for any one who cannot renounce home luxuries and comforts. Since, too, those Magyar grandees, whose brilliant genial hospitality gave Vienna her ancient social reputation, have, in consequence of political enmities, completely disappeared from the scene, the Tustige Wien has lost most of her traditional attractions in this kind. Then the remnant of society which still survives cleaves more closely than ever to the surprising machinery of the exclusive system, and shows, besides, a Chinese dislike of strangers. Thus the upper ten thousand—or, to speak by the card, the upper three hundred—are practically unapproachable by foreign interlopers who do not possess the open sesame of exceptional privilege. Hence no one now comes to Vienna either to save money or to disport himself in gilded saloons. On the other hand, despite the want of proper hotel accommodation at certain periods of the spring and autumn, the Graben and the Prater are almost as full of strangers as the Corso at Easter, or the Cascine at Whitsuntide. Then comes the British tourist, armed with the crimson strabo of Albemarle Street, which at once marks him out as a proper subject for imposture and extortion decorated with the favourite apparatus of straps, pouches, and other articles of ornamental saddlery, accompanied by a female train, whose rosy cheeks and rainbow toilettes excite the wonder of all the population. For energy and rapidity of performance he stands alone. He and his shove their way through the Kohlmarkt without apologising to the astonished persons for the thumps and pushes inflicted on the slow, courteous Austrians. They rattle through the Stefan's kirche, almost knocking down the acolytes, and drowning the litanies with their jabber. They rush into the vaults of the church of the Capucines, and, rattling their umbrellas on the silver coffins of twenty fossil Hapsburgs, chaff the guardians of these venerable relics of K. K. greatness, about the pleats of the historic Austrian lip. Then plunging into the depths of the Belvedere, they remark the vulgarity of Titian's Ecce Homo in comparison with Mr. Olman Unt's Light of the World, and the bad drawing of the acromion process in Rubens' snarling crocodile—that miserable Exaliosaurian so completely eclipsed by Turner's Dragon of the Hesperides.

Looking to the point of national pride, we may rejoice that the British tourist does not come to close quarters with the aristocracy of Austria. And yet if the contact could be, advantage would result to both sides; for as our country people might pick up manners, so the Austrians might pick up ideas. However, the business which specially concerns us here, is transacted in Vienna with a high degree of intelligence, and in this department of human excellence the English come in with the ruck of the European race. The Ball, as an institution, seems to be a distinguishing mark of the modern civilisation of the west. According to oriental notions the gasping and agitated movements of the dance degrade the dignity of the human person, and may not be publicly exhibited except by a professional class. A like notion prevailed in the Greek and Hebrew world. Turkish diplomacy has made concessions to European habits, so that the representatives of the Sublime Porte are permitted to give balls, and the younger Ottomans are sometimes tempted to indulge in a furtive waltz. But, as a rule, decent Easterns may not trip it on the light fantastic toe. In this respect, we of the west have surely chosen the wiser course. For, barring the incidental objection attaching to late hours, which are no necessary part of Terpsichore's practice, the ball is the most reasonable of social entertainments. Now that conversation has lost its salt, and that society is nothing but a hustling, hurrying crowd, it is better to go where music, dancing, truffles, and champagne await us, than to stiff gatherings of what Byron calls

'the polished horde
Formed of two mighty tribes, the bores and bored.'

For women balls may sometimes be full of disappointment and disgust, but they are the paradise of men. At balls the fair sex put on their best charms of manner, their finest attire, their most massive chignons, and, in a word, open all the batteries of female seduction. The general radiance of feeling and behaviour is diffused, even over those who do not partake in the special business of the night. Under such circumstances gossip forgets some of his twaddle, stiffness loses something of her starch, flirtation becomes a more spontaneous and more gushing flood. Especially is this the case amongst the Cephalopodous Viennese, whose brains seem to be located in their heels. There are striking spectacles of the ball sort to be seen in Vienna. The annual Gala Ball given at the Hofburg, and the public Bürger, or Citizens' Ball at the Redoubten Saal are of matchless splendour and outer interest. The social code of Austria, which is no less severe than the laws of the Medes and Persians, does not permit the close contact of plebeians with the nobility and K. K. Court. Sixteen quarterings on the shield, in other words, a double current of blue blood, at least eight generations, or a pedigree two hundred years long, are the warrant for admission to good society and the presence of the Imperial House. However, into the annual ball, even such profane vulgar as Cabinet Ministers, Members of Parliament, Foreign Ambassadors, and the like, are usually smuggled; so that the company present on these occasions swells in dimension and degrades in gentility to the English and French standards. The Burg is a plain, rambling palace of the barrack class, with staircases and approaches of analogous style, and devoid of positive decoration except carpets and whitewash. On a ball night the main streets of Vienna are choked by files of carriages and fiacres streaming up from every region of the city to the Franzens platz of the Burg. The entrance gained, an almost equally endless line of corridors, guarded by Heydries in the livery of the double eagle, leads to the first of a snaky series of apartments, which must be traversed before the Ritter Saal, or great hall of ceremony can be reached. The Saal is of spacious and lofty proportions encircled by a range of Corinthian columns, with an orchestral tribune at the extreme end, the whole construction being lined with white scagliola, and lighted from rows of burners set along the entablature below the ceiling. The company is arranged in horseshoe shape to await the coming of the Court. Down the sides of the Saal are benches rising in an amphitheatre fashion, and occupied by the ladies of the aristocracy, to whom, according to their respective rank, specific places are assigned. Below them stand the gentlemen of the Court, nobles, Hofraths, and other official staff, great military personages, and the officers of the regiments in garrison, besides strangers from the adjacent provinces of the empire; the curve of the horseshoe is formed by the foreign diplomatic body, the ambassadors with their respective suites standing just beneath the tribune, the ambassadors' wives and other official ladies, or female visitors of distinction, being close at hand. While the company gathers a hum of muffled conversation is heard; but the gaiety proper to the opening of a ball is chilled to the icy tone prescribed by palatial etiquette. At length something agitates the distant margin of the sea of heads; a way is cut through the close crowd as suddenly as if a battery of guns had opened fire upon its mass; a cloud of chamberlains, thrown out as skirmishers in advance, widen the lane into a road by civil entreaties, sugary threats, and the gentle pressure of their wands of office. The Imperial cortége advances in closer order, a blazing column of coloured uniforms embroidered with silver and gold, led by their Imperial Majesties in person. The company express their loyalty by profound obeisances, which are graciously acknowledged by the K. K. pair, who tread slowly and solemnly up the Saal, followed by their glittering retinue, till the ranks of the foreign ambassadors are reached. Here the Emperor falls off to greet the gentlemen of the diplomatic body, the Empress in like manner moving towards the female representatives of foreign countries. His majesty shakes hands with the ambassador who has been longest resident at his court, makes a few inquiries about the health of the royalty at home, with whom his excellency is assumed to be in close correspondence, and then pauses in order to allow the presentation of persons of the ambassadorial suite. Having asked every such individual whether his sojourn in Vienna pleases him—a question usually answered with a strong affirmative—his majesty proceeds to the latitude of the ambassador next in order, and repeats the same exciting ceremony. Afterwards he approaches the ministers-plenipotentiary, and then, with that grace of manner which is his most marked characteristic, addresses a few words of recognition to the gentlemen who have already had the honour of making his Imperial acquaintance. Royal memories, generally so empty of things, are usually guided by instincts in respect to persons, which seem little less than miraculous for accuracy and extent.

During this time the Empress gratifies, first the foreign ladies, then the foreign gentlemen, with a like exchange of compliments. As she advances with the tread which Virgil attributes to the queen of the gods, her face and figure full of commanding majesty and smiling grace, bowing to right and left with swan-like elegance of motion, a suppressed murmur of admiration runs through the great assembly. A few clouds of tulle, fastened with jewels that might furnish an empire's ransom, a nosegay of camellias mixed with hanging brilliants, an India of rubies and diamonds blazing through a coronet of lustrous brown hair—such are the adornments of this paragon of imperial creatures, the most beautiful of a beautiful Bavarian race. A soft, yet sorrowful voice, which addresses every stranger in his own language with rare purity of accent, intonation, and happy choice of words, completes the charms of this enchanting and right royal ravishment. When the formalities of presentation compliment are concluded, their majesties pass to the ranks of the domestic guests, where, however, they make but a short stay. This interlude finished, the orchestra strikes up, a space is cleared in front, and the Empress, accompanied by the archduchesses present, and the several ambassadresses, takes her place on a sofa to see the dancing. On these occasions, whether from the fear of doing irreparable damage to priceless tunics and flounces of Cluny and Valenciennes, or from the presence of that formidable army of unknown lookers-on, which gives the ball the publicity of a ballet, there is an absence of the *brio* proper to private assemblies, and a reluctance to step into the magic circle. The whole scene almost surpasses the splendours of operatic pageantry. No uniforms are so brilliant at night as those of Austria, nowhere else is there a finer flaunting of silks, brocades, and satins, nor a more glittering display of pearls, emeralds, and diamonds. There is not much beauty of a striking sort amongst the Austrian ladies, but their forms are well grown, and the younger people present the true type of aristocratic distinction, both in manners and appearance. Heaven generally bestows compensations on its creatures, and the Austrians, so empty of brains and knowledge, excel in dancing. The older people p e end that the adoption of steel petticoats and trailing skirts has caused a visible decline in the skilled practice of this delightful art, but a stranger is more likely to wonder at the perfection of the present than to sigh for the refinements of the past. Dancing, like singing, cannot be properly cultivated in narrow and crowded rooms, so that our own degraded style of execution may well be pardoned. Englishmen have rarely enough ear for music to recognize the difference of rhythm that separates the polka from the waltz, although they can sometimes detect, empirically, the jingle of a familiar tune. In Vienna it never happens that a dancing Dumdreary, after listening without result to an orchestral strain, is driven to inquire the nature of the dance about to be performed. The Viennese are not addicted to music of a high class, but their bearing is of the keenest, both for melody and time, wh never their perceptions are spurred by the stimulus of dancing. Jean Paul said every Englishman was an island and in like manner it may be said that every Englishman, and every English woman too, have their own way of dancing. Some dancers have no ear at all, the majority step without precision, one has a snaky slide, another a sparrowy hop, one likes a solemn andante, another a wriggling presto; this confident damsel clings close to her partner, that bashful virgin struggles as she moves to evade the impropriety of a too close embrace. Under such anarchical circumstances there is no chance for the development of a refined and congruous style of art. Then, as the education of the heels hardly satisfies the requirements of an English social career, our youth are too disposed to neglect this, the only vital branch of Austrian schooling. Thus it will be easily understood that Austrians dance with an elegance and ease which, amongst ourselves, has no existence at all.

The Emperor does not permit his guests to remain too late, so that before the stroke of midnight, gold stick, advancing to the imperial sofa, invites the imperial and diplomatic personages to come to tea. The Empress leading the van, the ladies whose rank gives them this exalted privilege follow her majesty across the Saal, through several corridors and apartments to the room specially prepared for the royal company. Her majesty takes her seat at a table with an ambassadress on one hand and an archduchess on the other, taking care that their tea is properly seasoned with sugar and milk. The gentlemen crowd into the room, and all eyes are directed to the beautiful hostess. Perhaps nothing but the habit of the stage can steel a woman to ordeals like this, which, if flattering to vanity, are terrible encounters even for the toughest nerves. No other sovereign in the bloom of youth and loveliness commands a larger stock of self-possession than the Austrian empress; but even she, on given occasions, seems to shrink from the admiration of her lieges with the conscious modesty of a woman who finds herself the cynosure of a thousand ardent eyes. At length the scene of trial closes, and the company return to the Saal to witness the final cotillon. Meanwhile, tables are spread throughout the adjoining rooms with tea, coffee, ices, jellies, preserves, cakes, and other light refreshments. Solid supper is not given, but champagne and punch flow in rivers on every side, and the imperial flunkeys distribute bonbons that transcend the choicest morsels of Boissier or Zouache. These luscious treasures are wrapped not in mere shreds of tinsel, but in artistic photographs of the members of the imperial family. Thus while the Austrian mouth is satiated with sugar, the Austrian mind is stimulated with loyal sentiment. At length the cotillon ends, the imperial pair retires, the company crowds the steps, and soon after midnight the last carriage rolls away from the entrance of the Burg.

Few private balls are given in the best Vienna circles; but some of those which do occur may be taken as models of sumptuous and refined hospitality. For the Austrians, who, in respect of every other species of social entertainment, are a churlish and close-fisted people, when a ball is on the tapis forget their parsimony and open their purses wide.

In Vienna there are are two private palaces justly famous for their balls. The town houses of the English aristocracy sometimes possess handsome apartments, but special ball-rooms are almost, if not quite, unknown. Paris and Petersburg can show many opulent and imposing mansions. For magnificence of internal plan and decoration the palaces of Rome are unapproached, and in many of them thought has been taken for great festive occasions. All these cities do honour to Terpsichore; and the Roman entertainments, in particular, are calculated to make a strong impression on æsthetic minds on account of the architectural beauty, the tapestries, the statues, the paintings, the superb proportions of the rooms where they are held. But the mere business of dancing is better transacted at Vienna. All the arrangements and appliances are well adapted to the one great end. The entrance-hall, the corridors, the main staircase, are lined with an army of liveried lackeys; and a long series of chambers, easy of approach and egress, lead to the ball-room, which is provided with several outlets, so as to prevent the circulation being stopped. The ball-room is spacious, lofty, faced with scagliola ornaments, imitated from good models of Rococo decoration, lighted with exceeding brilliancy by lustres of Vienna manufacture, which, as their framework is of wood, are able to be constructed of unusually massive proportions. The music is matchless, and consists either of executants from the orchestra of Strauss, or of a select military band. Strauss stands at the head of his art, and the Austrian bands seem scarcely to belong to the same instrumental category as those of England and France. The military music of Austria is a slave rather than a German institution, for the greater part of the performers are either Czechs, Hungarians, or Hungarian slaves. The bandsmen play with equal facility on wind and stringed instruments; and nothing can surpass their splendour of tone, their elaboration of finish in execution, the certainty and solidity of their *ensemble*. Lovers of music can never tire at an Austrian ball, and the most bigoted purist will find beauty of melody and treatment in the compositions performed. The mere operation of dancing is kept up till morning with great vigour, but other sorts of amusement do not prosper. Flirtation, in particular, does not seem to flourish on Austrian aristocratic soil. There are no tender couples sitting apart in cozy corners; no naughty princesses listening to declarations till their chaste cheeks blush with happiness or fear; no gay deceivers, entreating for surreptitious gloves, kisses, and locks of hair. That Austrian folly never grows romantic, that there exists no current of subterraneous sentiment, it would be rash to assert. But it may safely be said that outer demonstrations of such a sort are very rarely witnessed, and that the scandalous chronicle is very seldom invoked. Like other women, those of Vienna are asked and given in marriage, nor can it be supposed that an Austrian wedding is an invariable guarantee of matronly virtue. Still such business is transacted *sub rosa*, and flirtation, whether as a preliminary or a pastime, is not cultivated or comprehended in its artistic forms. Flirtation, after all, is a science that demands for its exercise a certain amount of intellectual resource, and the mildest minimum of thought is too heavy a tax on the Vienna brain. However, other intellectual compensations exist. The 'provant' department is administered with a completeness which would give Captain Dalgetty his heart's desire. After the first cotillon is ended, generally between two and three in the morning, supper is announced. A dancing archduke leads in the lady of the house, the other dancers follow with their partners; durchlauts and other dignitaries take a road and room apart.

The Austrians are large eaters, but quantity, not quality, is their test of culinary excellence. However, good cooks are to be found in Vienna at low wages by any one who takes the precaution of closing with a Czech or Hungarian artist; for Germans, as a race, are incapable of mastering the inner refinements of the culinary science. The cooks of Vienna excel in sweet dishes, and women who cannot brew a *potage Colbert* or *Bisque* will nevertheless turn out faultless *méringues*.

It is hard to get a good dinner at any of the hotels or traiteurs of Vienna. A small restaurant is attached to the casino, or aristocratic club, in the Herrengasse. Here the viands and wine, if falling far below the Parisian standard, though rather above the Parisian prices, are at least tolerable. The Austrians do not much indulge in dinner hospitality, so that the rising generation, which does not travel and does not study Brillat-Savarin, has no fair chance of educating its palate. At balls the greatest exertions are made, and the guests may always sup, if not wisely, at least well. This important meal cannot, of course, be taken standing by people of strict gastronomic principles. As the great object of Amphitryons and artists alike is to assimilate their suppers to those of Paris, to describe the savoury mountains under which the tables groan would be to re-edit the best pages of Francatelli and Ude. Perhaps the pride of Austrian larders is the Bohemian pheasant, a bird of fatter and more luscious flesh than his British cousin. The capercailzie, or auerhahn (*Tetrao urogallus*), is a fowl of splendid personal appearance, but indifferent culinary qualities. The capercailzie is to the grouse what the aurochs is to the race of domestic cattle, and from his size and eccentric habits he is much sought after by Austrian sportsmen. He must be caught in the act of whistling to his frau gräfin, in which pastime he only indulges at night. Then the sportsman, advancing with diplomatic precaution till the bird's form is seen in relief against the sky, kills this parent of our grouse as he sits perched on his bough anticipatory not of death but of flirtation. This may appear a poaching procedure, but the case of the wild swine in Austria is sadder still. In the imperial beast-garden, near Vienna, for instance, *sus ferox* roams about munching acorns, and keeping company with the K. K. deer, for the out-door species of Austrian hog is a sociable creature. Huts are erected at the points where the forest paths and glades intersect each other; and on the occasion of a grand battue Imperial Majesty, and as many of the eighteen archdukes as may be available, take their stations in the aforesaid huts. The peaceable and reluctant wild swine being then driven past in battalions, are satisfactorily slaughtered by breech-loaders till the vindictive humours of the ruler's soul have passed. Poor Austrian out-door hog! It is said that from motives of economy his beast-garden at Hutteldorff and elsewhere will be dismantled, so that ne will presumably be free to roam about the face of the empire. But hogs and capercailzies should only concern us in respect of their esculent properties.

Amongst the specialities of Austrian dancing-life should be mentioned the balls given in the many assembly rooms of the city. In addition to the so-called 'pic-nics' of the aristocracy, a sort of Austrian Almack's, there are public balls got up by and for specific classes of the population. For instance, the students, the tourists, the artists, the burghers, each of these classes has its separate ball. The artists' ball is the most interesting, as the celebrities of the *corps de ballet* appear and dance in the costume of ordinary life, arrayed, too, with a richness of silks, satins, and laces that cannot be surpassed by the most expensive efforts of aristocratic crinoline. The bürger ball is held in the Redouben Saal, an assembly-room belonging to the apartments of the Burg, and let out by the competent K. K. Beamten to individuals or committees. The great room is surrounded by a continuous gallery, from which the ladies of the aristocracy, who could not degrade themselves by contact with the dancers, watch the proceedings of the middle classes at the bürger ball. This ball offers an admirable bird's-eye view of the class in question. A stranger who visits it on two or three consecutive occasions will probably come to the conclusion that the amalgamation of the Austrian aristocracy and middle class will not be achieved until the latter make more show than they do at present of copying the outward appearance and manners of the former. It is hardly conceivable that anything short of a convulsion would throw the two orbits into one. However repugnant Austrian practice in this respect may be to English notions, it is doubtful if our ways would suit the banks of the Danube. While the nobles decline to stoop, the middle class does not much desire to climb. Far from the faults of the social strata being a source of bitterness to those below, they are accepted as harmless, if not useful, interruptions of a continuity which no one desires to establish.

RECOLLECTIONS OF A BACHELOR.

By Jack Easel.

TO be twenty years of age, with a sound digestion, a light heart, and a latch-key, seems to me, in certain moods, the *summum bonum* of earthly enjoyment. I am not going to remark that a man at that time of life is cleverer, or more virtuous, or a more profitable member of society than when his beard begins to grizzle. I only say he is happier: that he has probably never been so happy before, and that he certainly will never be so again. The jollity of schoolboys is, I fancy, over-rated. We look back upon that so-called golden period of early youth through a pleasant but deceptive halo, which makes us forget the alloy of discomforts which it contained. In the old Greek epigram, a certain hero hails with reverence both Mnemosyne and Lethe in one breath. 'Let me,' cries he, 'remember all the good I have done, and forget my errors.' And, after this fashion, we indulge in a retrospect of cricket and round jackets. We call to mind the delights of 'breaking-up day,' our unimpaired appetite for pastry, the glow of pleasure with which we received our prizes (you may guess how many fell to my share), but we forget the miseries we endured; the horrors of *Propria quæ maribus* and *Pons asinorum*; the fussy platitudes of that old pedagogue in a trencher cap; the brutal conduct of the young sixth-form tyrant for whom we had the honour of fagging; the depressing chill of early 'chapels;' the cruel scars which were left upon——: no; not even if Mr. Gunter himself were to offer me the whole contents of his shop bridecakes and all; not if I might be captain of the school eleven; not if I could read 'Euripides' as easily as the 'Times' newspaper; not for the rosiest cheeks in the world, the most generous 'tips' that could be hoped for,—nay, not to be that model of scholastic perfection, Mr. Thomas Brown himself,—would I go back to fifteen again!

But to call oneself *man* for the first time; to wield the razor with a consciousness of real necessity (boys used to shave in 184—); to live in lodgings or chambers on one's own account,—go out or come home when one likes; to enter upon life with a keen zest for life's enjoyments, with health, spirits, hope, and a tolerably easy conscience—ah! that is the true golden age; those are the rosy hours when, taking old Father Time kindly by the hand, setting his scythe and hour-glass in the chimney-corner, and passing the loving-cup across the table to him, most of us would cry, 'Here, venerable sire, here let us linger!'

I believe a common protest is raised from time to time, by old fogeys, that young men in this country are not what they used to be; and, upon my word, though I disregarded the notion a dozen years ago, I begin to have some faith in it now. One faculty, at least, they seem to be losing—the faculty of enjoyment.

Look at Young England in a ball-room, at the theatre, or during a pic-nic. Does he look happy, amused, or *impulsed* in any way? or is he a mere listless young dandy, *blasé*, and bored—or affecting to be so—with everything and everybody around him? I vow there are some young gentlemen of this description whom I never see without feeling a strong desire to slap them heartily between the shoulders (can't you imagine their horror at such a greeting?), and ask what on earth they think worth caring for. Early in the last *decennium*, we young fellows, whose whiskers were just beginning to bud, not only enjoyed life, but didn't mind showing that we enjoyed it. Our tastes were none of the most intellectual, I am afraid. We courted the muses after a rough and ready fashion—over pipes of bird's-eye and tankards of pale ale. There weren't so many novels to read then as there are now; but somehow I fancy they had better stuff in them. I know we looked forward every month to the appearance of Mr. Thackeray's two yellow leaves, and Mr. Dickens's two green leaves, with a zest which is unknown to the rising generation. There was not a chapter in 'David Copperfield' that we didn't discuss, laughing at Peggotty and Mr. Micawber, indignant with Uriah Heep, pitying poor little Dora, and deeply touched by the fate of handsome, reckless, proud, misguided Sturforth. Pendennis we voted somewhat of a prig; but his friend, George Warrington—was not *that* a character to study, to admire, and emulate? I believe when the great satirist of our day, in his profound world-wisdom, sketched that lifelike portrait, half the interest with which he invested it was due to the fact that he was unconsciously describing himself. Only a few of us had kept up our Latin; and Raikesmere, of the State Sinecures Office (who went up from Eastminster to Oxford, but left that university, for reasons which need not here be named, without taking his degree), was mighty apt with his quotations from Horace when we met at the Cimbrian Stores to dine, or sat gossiping round some third-floor fireplace in the Temple. 'Nunc est bibendum!' he used to cry, blowing off the froth from his pewter; and most of the young artists who heard him, not having themselves had the advantage, as the phrase is, of a classical education, regarded that thriftless reprobate as a miracle of wit and learning. But when we came to talk of books in our own mother-tongue—of English poets, from Chaucer down to Mr. Tennyson—my goodness, what a chattering there was! what a fierce puffing of threepenny cheroots! what an outpour of earnest, frank, and beer-inspired arguments!

The Cimbrian Stores was an old-fashioned tavern, where an eighteenpenny ordinary was held at six o'clock. The bitter ale (and a very decent tap too) came to fourpence, and one gave twopence more to the waiter, which, you see, exactly made up the two shillings—a modest but sufficient item in our daily expenses. I've had worse dinners in my time, I can tell you. They gave us soup or fish, a cut off the roast, vegetables, and a famous piece of Cheddar cheese. There was wine at a moderate tariff for those who liked it. Mr. Vokins, the respected landlord, took the chair precisely as the quaint old mahogany-cased clock in the corner struck the hour, and, rapping the table with his carving-knife, said a brief but impressive grace. It was a snug and cosy little set that gathered round that table. A few middle-aged personal friends of Mr. V. sat right and left of him. On the subject of their respective professions I was then, and am still, completely in the dark. They entered the room just five minutes before dinner-time, and fell half asleep over their grog, when we youngsters went back to our books and drawing-boards, or oftener, if my memory doesn't deceive me, to the pit of some theatre, especially in the winter season, when we made a point of visiting all the pantomimes.

I am thankful to say that I have not yet lost my relish for pantomimes. Burlesques, I admit, bore me horridly. It wasn't so with dear Planché's inventions. *His* wit was elegant and scholar-like; *his* jokes, if not profound, had a genuine sparkle about them quite independent of the mere *double entendre*; the stories which he chose for illustion were admirably adapted for his purpose. You didn't want a breakdown nigger dance, or an infant prodigy, or an optical illusion to set them off. The days of Vestris, the days of Harley, or Mdlles. St. George, Reynolds, and Horton,—*that* was the golden age of burlesque writing and burlesque acting. Those artists played their parts as if they enjoyed the fun themselves. Your modern actors and actresses seem only to condescend to theirs. They enunciate those wretched little milk-and-water puns as if they were ashamed of them—and well they may be, for, as a rule, weaker balderdash has never passed for wit. Jokes indeed! why you might make a gross of them in an hour. They are not jokes—they are not even puns—but a silly jingle of sounds. The audience don't laugh at this stuff: they can't. I defy any one with a grain of sense to do so. They only utter a dismal groan, which runs round the dress-circle like a banshee's wail.

But a pantomime, a real, genuine, well-organized pantomime, with a regular transformation scene and plenty of harlequinade, is a national institution which I trust may never become extinct. It is not an intellectual amusement, perhaps; to enjoy it you need be familiar neither with politics nor the pages of Dr. Lemprière's dictionary. It is simple nonsense, if you will—but then it pretends to be nothing else. We can't always (thank goodness) combine instruction with amusement, like the amiable pedagogues who invent geographical games, and playfully beguile little boys into the rule of three. No; a pantomime is solely intended to make us laugh, and the man who refuses to laugh at it once a year, and in the presence of children, must be a gloomy misanthrope. For my part I confess to no little sympathy with Mr. Merryman in his various escapades. I like to see him purloining sausages, geese, and legs of mutton, and admire the adroitness with which he transfers those comestibles to his capacious pocket. I am pleased when he divides the fish with Pantaloon, and, with a great semblance of fairness, reserves by far the larger share for himself. I rejoice when he is fired out of a cannon or pressed flat in a mangle, because I know by experience that his constitution can stand these trials, and that ten to one he will be livelier for them in the next scene. As for Columbine, I have always regarded her as one of the most fascinating women in Christendom, and could desire no better fate than to go through life with such a partner, pirouetting up and down the world dressed in a tight suit of spangles, like that lucky dog Harlequin, who can leap into a clock-face, or disappear through a shop-shutter as quick as lightning—whenever it suits his convenience.

A halo of intense respect surrounds the memory of those old Cimbrians as I picture them to myself, seated on sturdy Windsor chairs, in that homely but hospitable parlour panelled high with English oak, and bearing on its walls fair copies of the Lely portraits at Hampton Court. They were very strong in politics—those stout and ancient Britons—a subject which, judging from my own experience, interests the art-student but very little. So we let them say their say, and wag their venerable old heads with solemn earnestness, as they discussed the merits of Sir Robert Peel, and entered at length upon the great Chartist question.

As for *nous autres*, we kept our conversation pretty much to ourselves. Sometimes a dozen of us, painters, sucking barristers, government-office clerks, and a medical student or two, would form a little conclave at one end of the table, and, content for once to spend a quiet evening, would sit on, gossiping, long after the old *habitués* of the place (the *extra-ordinaries*, as we used to call them, in playful allusion to the nature of the banquet) had toddled home. It was at one o'clock, I think, when Robert, the head waiter, used to come in, rubbing his eyes, with a ' Now gentlemen, if you please!' the usual form of warning which he gave us previously to turning off the gas. I fear a good deal of what military men call 'pipeclay,' and civilians 'shop,' was talked on all sides, and the artists had the best of it. It will, I believe, be admitted that the failing is natural to us as a class. Scarcely any other calling can be said to furnish a theme for work and play to the same devotees. When Mugwell, the rising young lawyer, goes off to Switzerland for the long vacation, do you suppose he troubles his head with Blackstone on the Wengern Alp, or pops a brief into his pocket before stepping on board the boat at Lucerne? You might travel all day with those eminent medical celebrities, Dr. Pillington and Mr. Lancelot Probus, and never find out that one gentleman obtained a livelihood by writing hieroglyphics at a guinea a page, and that the other would be ready at any moment to cut you up—not metaphorically, but in the flesh—without the slightest remorse? I have known even sober and unimpeachable divines modify their costume to no small extent as soon as they have crossed the Channel, exchange the conventional white choker for an easy silk neckerchief, replace the stern chimneypot with a comfortable wideawake, and wear an ordinary shooting-coat instead of the more orthodox paletot. Barring a slight tendency to intone his conversation, you would hardly recognize his reverence in the frank and genial talker who sits next you at the table d'hôte. If our young clergy have their little failings they certainly do not intrude ecclesiastical intelligence upon you between the wine and walnuts, that is, unless you begin the subject. But what does an artist like to talk about so much as his art? How delighted he is sure to be if, agreeing with the theories which he propounds, you endorse his opinion that Madder Brown is a great genius! With what mingled pity and contempt he will regard you if you happen to admire the landscapes of Stippler! 'What, my dear fellow, *that* man's work like nature? Nonsense! I tell you there isn't a bit of nature in it! It's the feeblest, most commonplace stuff you ever saw! I don't suppose he ever drew anything but a cork correctly in all his life! Colour, indeed! the fellow's got no sense of colour in him. That foreground of his thing last year—hung on the line too, by Jove!—was nothing but a sheer piece of cabbage from Fogley's picture, and as for his greens—' &c., &c.

The artist-diners at the Cimbrian Stores outnumbered all the others put together. Law and medicine held their own sometimes; and when the gossip turned on general literature, we met on common ground. But art was the favourite subject of conversation, or 'jaw,' in the polite language of the Cimbrians. Our occasional visitors, perhaps, found it a little too much of a good thing sometimes, but most of them were very good-tempered on this point, and listened in meek astonishment to the astounding expressions of sentiment which came pouring forth from our lips in a fragrant cloud of tobacco. Once, and once only, was there any marked or offensive allusion to this habit, when that muff, Raikesmere, would insist on bringing his friend, young Tuftleigh Hunter, also of the S-nec-re Office, to dine with us. The idiot came in evening dress, with a jewelled shirt-front, and looked round upon our tweed coats and hairy faces with a mixed look of surprise and contempt. We were civil enough to him at first, but he scarcely deigned to speak to one of us, and, winking at Raikesmere after dinner (he had been drinking pretty freely), remarked that there was a d—d smell of paint in the room. I don't think any one of us would have seen the allusion, but that the fool began to chuckle (as fools will) when he had uttered this splendid piece of witticism.

I was sitting just opposite him, and my old schoolfellow, Dick Dewberry, of the Middle Temple, was by my side. Dick had been at Oxford with Tuftleigh, and knew his line. Moreover, Dick was an amateur painter of no inconsiderable merit, and had a fellow-feeling for our cause.

'I beg your pardon, sir,' cries Mr. Dewberry, very stiffly, across the table; 'I think you said that——'

'That there was a smell of paint. Yes, I did,' says the grinning dandy; 'perhaps you don't object to it?'

'To which, sir, the paint or your remark?' asks Dick, pretty smartly.

Raikesmere turned crimson.

''Pon my life I don't know,' drawled Hunter. 'You seem to take offence. Are you a painter?'

'Why, no, sir, but I'm a gentleman,' cries Dick, lighting his cigar; 'and a few of my friends here are both.'

'Then I s'pose you're accustomed to paint,' sneers Hunter, unabashed.

Raikesmere was nudging his elbow, and telling him to shut up.

'Perhaps so,' retorts Dick; 'but there are some things we are *not* accustomed to, and don't mean to endure. Raikesmere, if your friend wants the fresh air, there's plenty of it down stairs in the street.'

Tuftleigh, pouring out another glass of wine, muttered something about a public room being public property, and that he'd be blanked before he moved to oblige anybody. He was getting rapidly drunk. Dewberry rang the bell.

'Robert,' said he, when the waiter made his appearance, 'is the billiard-room engaged?'

'Not a soul but the marker in it, sir,' says old Bob.

'Very well. Then what do you say to a game of pool, gentlemen?'

We all started up, glad of the opportunity to avoid a row, and left this uncivilest of civil servants alone with his friend. Raikesmere came after us with an ample apology, but it was the last time he ventured to bring one of his dandiacal acquaintances to dine with us.

'Confounded puppy!' growled Dewberry, when he had got back to his chambers; 'I wish I had punched his head. I would if he could have stood up and taken care of himself. There's no love lost between us, I promise you.'

'Ever seen him before?' I asked, for I felt sure there was some old grudge rankling in Mr. Dewberry's bosom.

'Well, yes, I have,' said Dick, somewhat mysteriously. 'He was pointed out to me at the Crystal Palace last Thursday.'

'By whom?' said I.

Mr. Dewberry blushed a little, and, in reply, asked me whether I could keep a secret.

'To be sure, especially when a lady is in the case,' I said, for the honest fellow had turned as red as a peony, and I saw at once that we were on delicate ground.

'The fact is, Jack,' continued D. D., 'that that fellow has been annoying a very great friend of mine for some time past, and in such a way that it would be very awkward, and, in fact, almost impossible for her—you're right, it *is* a lady—or for me, on her behalf, to take any notice of it.'

I now ventured to ask for a full explanation, having in the meantime mixed myself a glass of toddy, at Mr. Dewberry's express desire.

'You must know, then,' said Dick, after a pull at his own tumbler, 'that I have some friends living at Kensington, not far from where this fellow, Hunter, lives. In fact, they attend the same church of St Didymus. Their pew is in one of the aisles, and he generally manages to get a seat close by. Well, fancy, for some weeks past the horrid snob has been in the habit of staring in an impudent manner every Sunday during service at this lady, who is very young, you know, Jack, and — ahem! — really very pretty; and she hasn't any father or brother, by the way—yes, by Jove! in such a manner as really to annoy her very much, and she has 'tried to frown him down, but he won't be frowned down, and keeps on staring worse than ever. Now isn't it a disgusting shame, and don't you think it ought to be put a stop to in some way or another?'

'Most decidedly,' said I. 'Couldn't you call him to account yourself, or send a message by Raikesmere?'

'Why, no,' cries Dick; 'that's just the rub. I'd do that directly if I might, but Miss Petworth won't let me; and when one comes to think of it, you know, Jack, it would be rather awkward to mix a lady's name up with such an affair at all; because, of course, he'd deny that he meant to be rude, and say it was an accident, or something of that kind, and so get off without receiving his deserts. I want to teach him a lesson which he shan't forget in a hurry.'

'Well, what do you propose?' I asked.

'Why,' continued Mr. Dewberry, 'I've been thinking the matter over lately, and I see only one way of tackling it. It appears that Mr. Hunter's rudeness is not confined to one object. He has annoyed other ladies in the same way. Now I don't like the notion of anonymous letters, but really in a case of this kind I think the end would justify the means. He seems to be such a donkey, that I really think if he received a letter written in a woman's hand he would believe it came from one of those ladies whom he is always ogling, and then we could make as much fun of him as we chose.'

'I confess I don't exactly see how,' said I.

'Why, you old stupid,' cries Dick, 'don't you see that a man of this kind would be vain enough to keep any appointment anywhere, from the top of the monument to the bottom of the Thames Tunnel, in the fond belief that a lady had fallen in love with him, if he thought he was going to meet her. Supposing the rendezvous chosen was the Temple Gardens——'

'And you prepared with a tremendous horsewhip, I suppose,' said I.

'Why, no,' retorts Mr. Dewberry, 'that wouldn't be exactly fair—to inveigle a man, cad as he is, into a quiet place, and then lick him at one's leisure. No; I'm not going to do that. But there's nothing in the world to prevent his becoming a fund of amusement to us as he struts about waiting for his imaginary Dulcinea, while we are quietly watching and laughing at him from these windows.'

'Capital notion, upon my word,' observes Mr. Dewberry's humble servant. 'But it's easier said than done. Mr. Hunter mayn't be quite such a fool as he looks.'

'We can but try,' answers D. D 'Suppose we put out a bait to begin with. We might sketch out a preliminary note, asking him to give evidence of the sincerity of his affection in some sign which I should be able to recognize.'

'And when are these documents to be drawn up?' I asked.

'There is no time,' said Mr. Dewberry, fetching an inkstand from a side table, 'like the present.'

Down we sat accordingly, and in the course of half an hour the following billet was indited in a delicate female hand, on a sheet of superfine Bath post.

'SIR,—The experience which a nature such as *yours* must ere this have derived from a contemplation of the confiding impulses to which *a woman's heart* is occasionally subject may, I *trust*, be deemed some excuse for the exceptional character of this communication. It were impossible for me to witness *week* after *week* the *flattering*, because *unsolicited*, attention with which you regard the writer of these lines without becoming aware that you take an interest in her welfare which has not been—may I say—altogether *unappreciated*? Should my *suspicions*—I had nearly written my *hopes*—be not without foundation, will you kindly oblige me by wearing a pea-green tie (my favourite colour) round your neck on Sunday next? After seeing it I shall feel free to tell you *more*.

'Till then I remain,

'Your *unknown friend*,

'BELINDA.

'P.S. Isn't Belinda a pretty name? I'm afraid you won't think mine half so pretty *when you know it!*'

'By Jove I don't think he would if he *did* know it,' says Dick, laughing. 'Capital note upon my word, in the best style of a Complete Letter-writer, with plenty of underlining. If he believes *that*, he will deserve anything he gets. Of course next Sunday I shall go to St. Didymus and see if the bait has taken.'

'Do you intend to tell the young lady?' I asked.

'Not a word, my dear fellow, not a word,' said Dick, 'and for the best possible reason, that she would highly disapprove of the whole proceeding. Besides, what good would it do? At present the note may have come from any one of the girls to whom he has "made eyes." But if I told Miss P—— she would certainly betray herself by blushing or showing some confusion next Sunday, and then the whole thing would be spoiled. No, I must not compromise her in any way. What a jolly sell it will be, though, for him, if he falls into the trap! Can't you fancy him in his pea-green tie? I chose that colour because he usually wears crimson silk.'

Well, a week after the above conversation Dick and I met again at his chambers by appointment. He told me that Mr. Hunter had obeyed the request so literally that he thought if we had begged him to wear a bonnet instead of a hat we might have expected compliance. The time was now come for a second letter, which was couched in the following elegant language.

'SIR,—How can I express to you in adequately *earnest* terms the great satisfaction, nay, the *pleasure*, which I felt in recognizing on your part, through the medium of a sign which I *myself* had suggested, an evidence of what, until I *knew* it, I did not dare to anticipate? I am going with my aunt (an old maid, very kind in *her way*, but unfortunately indifferent to the feelings of *young people*) into the City on Tuesday next, and I will try to be in the Temple Gardens between two and three in the afternoon. I know it is indiscreet in me to say this, but I feel *confident* that I can rely on your *secrecy* and good faith. Perhaps I may be enabled to tell you this in *person*, but if not I am sure you will believe

'Your unknown but *sincere* friend,
'BELINDA.

'P.S. If I am unfortunately detained until four or half-past you won't mind, will you? What a lovely colour that pea-green tie was, and *how well it became you!* Of course *I* couldn't *with propriety* take any notice of *you*, but I felt conscious that you had not forgotten *me*.'

'I'm afraid he'll see through it,' said Dick, as he folded up the letter. 'However, old fellow, you'll turn up here at any rate on Tuesday, and we'll keep a look-out for the young gentleman.'

* * * *

On Tuesday, the —th of January, 185- (you see I purposely refrain from giving the date in full, out of consideration for Mr. Tuftleigh Hunter's feelings, as he may, for aught I know, by this time be married, and have become the father of a family: if so, it will be far better for Mrs. T. H.'s happiness if she remains in ignorance of her husband's antecedents), on this bleak and frosty winter's day, as I was saying, two young and not altogether ill-favoured Englishmen might have been seen ensconced behind the ample folds of a red curtain which decorated a window in one of those quaint but historically interesting windows that command a view of the Temple Gardens. A pile of calf-bound tomes piled in careless confusion on an adjoining table indicated the legal studies in which one at least of the striplings was ostensibly engaged. But the remains of an unexceptionably grilled steak, and of what had once been a symmetrical pyramid of mashed potato, flanked by a tankard of foaming stout would have inspired the most careless observer with a conviction that both these young gentlemen had lunched, while a recently-opened box of cigars, and a delicious perfume which hung upon the noonday air, suggestive of the well-known Havannah plant, might have been accepted in evidence that the less necessary but more refined wants of civilized life were being amply satisfied.*

'How goes the time, Jack?' asked Mr. Dewberry, blowing rings of smoke out of an elegantly-carved meerschaum pipe. 'I let my watch fall in the racket-court, yesterday, and broke the mainspring, I think.'

'Ten minutes past two,' said I, after consulting my own chronometer.

'Then I give him up,' said Dick, rather gloomily; 'but hark! what is that striking now? You're a little fast, I believe, like some of my other friends. It is but just two o'clock, and—hallo, why there he is, I declare. Punctuality is not only the soul of business, but the very quintessence of confiding affection: and I say, my dear Jack, *do* look here,' adds Mr. Dewberry, bursting into a roar of laughter, 'I'm hanged if he hasn't sported the pea-green tie, as a delicate attention. Ah! my exquisite Mr. Tuftleigh, I really begin to pity you. This *is* verdant with a vengeance.'

It was too true. The misguided young man had appeared in full fig, and clad after a manner anything but suited to the inclemency of the weather, in order, I presume, to show off his figure to the best advantage. He was walking about with the air of a stage gallant, evidently rejoiced that he had arrived before his *inamorata*. After he had strolled up and down for about a quarter of an hour, however, he pulled out his watch and began to walk quicker, and no wonder, for it was intensely cold. Another interval, somewhat shorter than before, having elapsed, the elegant Tuftleigh again ascertained the time, and, to make assurance doubly sure, referred to a piece of paper which he drew from his coat-pocket, and which we felt

* The composition of this last paragraph is not, I admit, in my usual style. But it is a style which, at the period referred to, found so much favour among a certain class of English novel readers that I felt an irresistible temptation to imitate it to the best of my humble ability.

convinced was the letter that had lured him to his fate. Mr. Dewberry and I, who watched these proceedings with unremitting attention (except, indeed, during the brief moments in which we reapplied ourselves to bottled stout), could not help remarking that the longer Mr. Tuftleigh stayed, the more frequently he looked at his watch, and the oftener he looked at his watch the further he extended his walk up and down. At last it began to grow dark, and Mr. Tuftleigh (we could see) began to grow impatient. He quickened his pace, stamping on the ground as he went, and warming the upper part of his frame after the fashion of London cabmen, who in winter time appear to be perpetually rehearsing with great vehemence the embracing of imaginary friends At last, when it was becoming almost too dark to see anything, Mr. Tuftleigh disappeared, after having afforded us infinite amusement.

'Well, what is the next thing to be done?' said Mr. Dewberry, after the half-hour had struck, and our hero had disappeared. 'Do you think he'd stand another letter?'

'I should hardly think so; but you know best, Dick,' said I.

After a short consultation we wrote another note, with many apologies from the fair unknown, stating that her aunt had disappointed her, and that she had been unable to make her way that afternoon towards the Temple Gardens, but promising faithfully to be there the following Friday at the same hour, hoping to meet her correspondent, to whom she (of course) owed ten thousand obligations, &c. &c.

I must confess that Mr. Hunter showed a sound discretion in taking no notice of the last epistle. But we could not allow the matter to drop here. It was absolutely necessary to put the ingenuous youth on his guard for the future. He had been allowed to take an unconscious part in this little farce. It now remained for us to read him the moral.

Letter No. 3 was in these words.

'Sir,—Your disregard of 'Belinda's' last assignation is tolerably good evidence that you are now aware how completely her first appointment made you the victim of a well-deserved hoax.

'You have for some time past been in the habit of annoying more than one lady by a species of rudeness which is all the more cowardly because it is difficult to define or bring home to you, and that, too, at a time and in a place which render your offence doubly inexcusable. Without entering into further particulars it is sufficient for you to know that these ladies have found a champion in one who, sorry as he would be to proceed to extremities, will assuredly take an early opportunity of calling you to account in a practical and not very pleasant manner if you have the temerity, after this warning, to continue your impertinencies. And, believe me, nothing but my desire to save these ladies from further annoyance has saved you, up to this time, from the chastisement which you richly deserve. It is scarcely necessary for me to add that they are quite unaware of the means which I have thought fit to adopt for their protection.

'I have the honour to be, sir,
'Your most obedient servant,
'A ROD IN PICKLE.'

The effect of this last epistle was so satisfactory that Mr. Tuftleigh Hunter ceased to frequent the church of St. Didymus entirely, and I trust has since abstained from the offensive practice of ogling altogether. That ladies, especially when they happen to be young and pretty, are not utterly averse to being looked at with respectful admiration I candidly admit. Indeed, judging from my own experience, I have always found that——, but there, I won't go on further. You see, I'm turned of thirty, and the subject awakens sentiments in my heart which lead me to decline revealing *all* the Recollections of a Bachelor!

A WEEK IN A COUNTRY HOUSE.

WHEN the London season is over, and the dying notes of the session become distinct, all the world rushes off hither and thither to obtain relief from the trammels of London life, or to repair the ravages of late hours at watering-places at home or abroad, or to enter into all the healthy pursuits of a country life, and enjoy the relaxation which they afford, or to comply with the rules of fashion, which prescribe that no one who aspires to the distinction of belonging to the fashionable world can remain in town after a certain time, and also retain his reputation and position as a member of that most exclusive circle. There is nothing more absurd than the extent to which some persons bow to the decrees of fashion. Instances are by no means rare in which persons who have been detained in London by some unforeseen necessity or by accident during the 'recesses' of Easter or Whitsuntide, have been known to draw down their blinds or shut their shutters, and live in some remote or back part of their house, that they may be supposed to have complied with the usages of 'society,' and to have left London for their 'seat in the country.' When Rotten Row is no longer frequented, and the throng of carriages in Bond Street and Regent Street is so diminished as not to interfere with the traffic nor peril the lives of the passers-by, and a certain carelessness in the arrangements of the shop-windows betray the fact that the rich and idle are gone beyond the reach of their temptation, country houses become in their turn the centres of festivities and of that social intercourse which knits families together. During the most bewitching time of the year the claims of the country have been overlooked, and it is therefore but fair that they should be recognized at last. In London 'society' is so *exigeant* in her demands upon those who go in for it' that people become her slaves, lose much of their individuality, and are utterly unlike themselves. Few people can withstand the ordeal of a London life. The ceaseless round of dissipation and the multitude of interests, great and small, which constitute its claims, are so engrossing, that the instances are rare in which the same aspect is maintained in town and country. None are made to feel this more keenly than country cousins who come up to London, at rare intervals, for a short time to see the sights and hear the news, in the expectation of finding their friends equally interested in them and their affairs, as devoted to them as ever, and willing to resume the thread of their intercourse where it had been broken off. Vain expectation! Every one knows that in a vast metropolis like London, society is divided and subdivided into a multitude of different cliques or circles, and that each one is distinct from the others, and that every one who lives outside any particular circle is as much an alien to it as if he lived in Japan. Hence it arises that country cousins do not find themselves on the same level with their relations to whom they are an invaluable acquisition in the country, and by whom they are *fêted*; but seem suddenly to have dropped out of the mind and heart of those who suffer themselves to be engrossed and carried away by the rapid whirl of a London season. London fine ladies and gentlemen are quite a class *sui generis*. They live in a world of their own, obey a law of their own, and speak a language of their own. Excitement follows excitement, and anything like comfortable and rational intercourse is scarcely known among those who give themselves up entirely to the claims and usages of society. It is in country houses, where there is less of that exclusiveness which prevails in London, and is its bane, that we must look for that interchange of thoughts and ideas which makes society pleasant. We do not, of course, pretend to deny that London contains within itself all that is necessary to constitute the most agreeable society in the world.

Where so much talent and such varied gifts are collected together it could not be otherwise; but we maintain that, as a rule, the fashionable world is not the soil in which that highest order of intellectual gifts flourishes, nor the atmosphere which is the most conducive to its free expansion Although every country house has its own especial friends, and its *habitués* belong more or less to a particular class, there is more geniality, more reality, more thoroughness in the intercourse. It is more earnest, more human, and therefore pleasanter and more satisfactory. It is not the same hollow, outside work which goes on in London, and it is as well that there should be seasons of interruption to that kind of life which fosters what is artificial, and must in the end stifle nature.

It was after a season of unusual gaiety, that Mrs. D—— and her son left London and went on their own devices to recruit or amuse themselves. Mrs. D—— went, in the first instance, to the seaside to restore the colour to her faded cheeks and renovate the strength which had been impaired by what she considered to be the duties she owed to society. She was a devoted mother, and her chief thought and study was how to advance the interests of her well-beloved son, Arthur; but she managed with considerable tact and cleverness to combine this with providing for herself as much amusement as she could enjoy. Arthur duly appreciated his mother's gifts and talents, which were considerable, and had always secured for her a ready admission to the best society; nor was he less touched by her devotion to himself. Under her protecting wing he had become a welcome guest in many pleasant houses, and Mrs. D—— showed her worldly wisdom and *savoir faire* when at her instigation they parted company for a time with a mutual understanding to keep each other *au courant* of all that happened. Their letters became a source of the greatest amusement to them. Their position, age, and circumstances, as well as the different society into which they went, secured for them the greatest variety of incidents, which they were well able to make the most of.

It was not long after Mrs. D—— had left Brighton, where she devoted herself exclusively to the care of her health, that she yielded to the many pressing invitations which she had received from her old friends the Garringtons. The Garringtons were pleasant people; they were hospitable, and knew how to make the best use of the appliances within their reach. They had children in abundance, of all sizes and ages, and two grown-up daughters, who were among the most popular girls in Belgravia, were the immediate cause of those dinners and concerts and *thés dansantes* for which the Garringtons had made themselves famous. These young ladies were always surrounded by a knot of *Cavalières servantes*, who were ever ready to fetch and carry, but these retrievers were for the most part poor, younger sons studying at the bar. However, Lady Garrington was not disquieted on their account, for she had too much confidence in her daughters' common sense, and in the principles she had inculcated, to have the slightest fear of their making a wrong move in the game of life which lay before them. Our friend Mrs. D—— was a great acquisition in a country house, for she possessed a fund of good humour, was always ready to be of use, had a remarkable talent for conversation, as well as other resources, which made her the life and soul of whatever society she frequented. It was soon after her arrival at Garrington Manor that she sat herself down to write to 'her boy,' as she always called her son. Her letters were more or less of a journal, but as they are descriptive of the scenes in which she played so conspicuous a part, we will let them speak for themselves.

' MY DEAR BOY,—Your mother has so much confidence in your care for number one that she will not begin her letter in the old style, "this comes hopping you are well as it leaves me;" but I will tell you my adventures since I left the Pall Mall of the seaside. Here I am at last at Garrington Manor, after the many pressing invitations which I have till now left unheeded. It was by no means a difficult journey, which, however, Rachel' (her maid, ED. L. S.) 'made even less difficult than it would have been, for her pretty face captivated guards and porters to such a degree that we received the greatest consideration and attention from them, and I doubled it down in my memory as a thing to be remembered that elderly women who are addicted to travelling about should secure the attendance of a pretty girl as lady's maid. On my arrival at the station I found everything ready for the removal of myself, bag and baggage, to the Manor; and when we arrived at the door a bevy of the most polite and obsequious servants awaited me, hastening to relieve me of my inseparable bag, and assuring me that Lady Garrington had been anxiously expecting me. Before I could turn round I found myself greeted in the warmest manner possible by my lady, who would insist upon my coming to her own room and having some tea (she knew my weak point), away from all the racket and noise which the young people were said to be making over croquet on the lawn. After sufficient time had been allowed for Rachel to unpack, I took refuge in my own room, having ascertained at what hour I was expected to make my appearance. I found Rachel in high glee, getting over her duties with wonderful alacrity, from which I inferred that she had again made a favourable impression, and that men are the same everywhere. You know I always like to be in time, and hate rushing down at the last moment into the midst of a crowd of people whom I don't know; so when Rachel had turned me off to her satisfaction, and I had been properly got up *à quatre épingles*, I descended to the drawing-room and found that I had it all to myself. Presently, however, the door opened, and a handsome youth, whom I had never seen before to my knowledge, sauntered in. It would be incorrect to say he walked in, it would be more true to say he rolled himself in. We looked at each other, and the handsome youth seemed to grow afraid of me, for instead of approaching the part of the room where I sat, he rolled himself on towards the window, while he drew a cambric handkerchief from his pocket and tenderly smoothed his young moustache. Again the door opened, and a fair and pretty girl tripped in, looking light and airy as a gossamer. She came towards me; I rose, we curtseyed, we squiddled, and said a few nothings to each other, and then the handsome youth began to thaw in the presence of beauty, and we all talked together of *la pluie et le beau temps* till the gong sounded, and many steps were heard approaching, and the Brownes and the Whites and the Garringtons all flocked in and greeted me. At dinner the handsome youth sat on my right and Beauty next to him. He was supercilious, and she listened devoutly to his dull platitudes, and I speculated upon how small an amount of thoughts and ideas, when in combination with *beaux yeux* the tender passion can take root in and exist. Well, all things come to an end, and so did my first evening at Garrington Manor, which I was not sorry for.

'The next morning, after having given special directions to Rachel to have my room ready as soon as she could, that I might write my letters, I went down to breakfast, and, to my dismay, found the whole party assembled, busily engaged in discussing their breakfast, but in almost solemn silence. The Garringtons, *père et mère*, were absorbed in their letters, while the rest waited patiently for such scraps of news as were vouchsafed to them at intervals. It was a solemn affair, and I became more convinced that it would be a wiser custom for people to eat their breakfast in their own rooms and not appear in public till they had been sustained and fortified by it. However, my late entrance created a diversion. I found your letter on my plate and put it into my pocket after I had satisfied myself that you were all right. No sooner was breakfast over than I found myself seized upon by the second Garrington girl, who entreated me to go with them. "Where in the name of heaven am I to go?" I inquired, thinking all the while that I had only just come, and longing to be quiet in my own room. After having quelled Miss Helen's energetic entreaties by an assurance that I would do whatever was required of me, I found myself engaged to go to Vere Abbey, a beautiful old ruin. I was told, where it was proposed to have a pic-nic. You know my horror of pic-nics, where people try their best to make themselves as uncomfortable as they can under the pretence of amusing themselves. The handsome youth was attacked by Beauty with numberless inquiries whether he could make a fire of damp sticks and boil a kettle, and I was amused at his look of consternation. However, there is no use in contending with the inevitable, so I quietly acquiesced and came down at the appointed hour duly equipped. The handsome youth and I began to fraternise, and I could not deny myself the malicious pleasure of teasing him by assuming that pic-nics were his *métier*, and that we all looked to him for help under the host of probable difficulties which I described as vividly and painfully as I could, while he sat on thorns at the prospect before him. When the carriages came round we were not long in arranging and disposing of our party. We all tried to be as merry as we could, and, luckily for us, the sun shone out brightly. After lionising Vere Abbey, which is really a beautiful ruin belonging to the old family of the De Veres, we disposed of ourselves according to our inclinations, and the whole party was scattered here and there, on the understanding that at a given time all should reassemble for luncheon. I had fortunately brought my drawing-book and prepared to sketch the ruin, when I was interrupted by some of the younger Garringtons, who assured me they delighted in nothing so much as watching a person draw. "Had I any colours? Oh! yes, I see, there they are. May we look at them?" A thousand questions were asked about what colours made what shades. "Had I a spare sheet of drawing-paper? Would I let them have it?" To all of which I was as complaisant as possible, and soon I saw my colour-box in a mess, my brushes saturated with water and paint, the spare sheet daubed over, and in despair I gave up the attempt on finding that I was expected to give a drawing lesson to my young friends, who ran off the moment luncheon-time drew near, leaving me to tidy it all as best I might. Then followed luncheon, when we sat on the damp grass or on the carriage-cushions, eating cold chicken and pies and salad, which is always on such occasions associated in my mind with slugs and earwigs. After the cravings of hunger had been satisfied we dispersed again, while the servants regaled themselves and packed up the knives and forks, &c., when we were hurried off, Lady G—— in despair that it was already so late, as a party of neighbours were expected to dinner, and unless we made great haste there would be scarcely time to dress, which was a subject of the greatest importance in Lady G——'s estimation. We did arrive, and, happily, before the invited guests, so Lady G—— was tolerably composed, and with hasty glances at the clock we all rushed off to get ready for dinner. Rachel is invaluable at a pinch, and I was among the first to reach the drawing-room; but what with the sun, the drive home, and the hurry of dressing, I felt scorched and anything but comfortable. However, it was all part of the play, and I was in for it. We were in no lack of subjects for conversation. Vere Abbey, its past history and its present state, was a safe subject, and you will be glad to hear that your mother did not, as you say, "put her foot into it." She was wonderfully cautious and circumspect, and I am sure earned for herself the reputation of being the most matter-of-fact of dames. As far as I was concerned all would have gone on smoothly enough but for one *contretemps*. Something, I don't know what, perhaps I had caught cold from sitting on the damp grass, or some spiteful fly may have provoked my nose; anyhow something made me sneeze, and in the greatest hurry I had recourse to my pocket handkerchief, when to my dismay I found it was the one which I had had in the morning, and which in my hurry I had caught up and put into my pocket. It was all over paint, thanks to my young would-be artist friends.

'The handsome youth looked at me with astonishment, and then burst into a loud fit of laughter. Beauty was startled at such an unwonted exhibition, and inquired into the cause, which he was quite unable to explain; and I, seizing the bull by the horns, declared myself to be the innocent occasion of it, and, making a sign to him not to betray me, kept them all for some time on the tiptoe of curiosity, which I at last gratified, when they seemed to me to be vastly disappointed that it was nothing worse.

'The next day I thought I should have to myself; so I planned exactly what I would do, and again gave Rachel strict injunctions to have my room got ready as soon as possible. After breakfast was over, and I had seated myself in my chair, and had collected round me all that I needed, I began to comfort myself with the thought that I should have, at all events, an hour or two to myself, when I heard a gentle tap at the door, and a lovely child with golden hair came in, inquiring whether she might come and sit with me a little while, as her sisters and the governess were gone into the village, and her mamma had said that if she could find Mrs. D——, she was sure she would tell her some stories; and mamma says no one can tell a story as well as you. "Will oo tell me one?" added she, imploringly. Who could resist such an appeal? So I looked at my books and my pen and ink, and all my preparations, and again surrendered myself to the inevitable, but not without a sigh. I moved to the open window, placed my young friend on a chair by my side, and began my story; when again another tap at the door, and another child came in search of her sister, and entreated that she, too, might be allowed to remain and listen to the story. No one ever had better listeners, so I ought to have been satisfied. I had nearly finished my task, when another knock at my door interrupted us, and the eldest of the sisters came to say that her mother wished me to come and sit with her in her room, till luncheon-time, if I was not otherwise engaged. At the entreaty of my young friends, I wound up my story and complied with Lady Garrington's request. So that morning was gone, and the afternoon was devoted to another excursion, after which we were all expected to play at croquet till dressing time. The next day it was the same thing over again. I got up earlier than usual, to write one or two letters which I could not put off, and after breakfast again took refuge in my room, in the hope of a few moments' peace, which I thought I had secured, for I began a letter to you, which I hoped I might finish before post-time; but at about half-past eleven I was interrupted by a tap at my door, and the door was slowly opened by the eldest daughter, who "hoped she did not disturb me," that I was not particularly engaged, because "mamma" had sent her to ask whether I would make a sketch of her. She already had one which I had done, of her eldest son, who was then with his regiment in India, and she would so like me to do one of her; and she went on to ask whether I would object to Beauty's coming too, to watch how I did it. Of course I was only too glad to be of use, and begged her to go and fetch her friend Beauty, while I got my materials ready. So, in sheer vexation of spirit, I put the letter I had begun to you into the fire, and got my paper, and chalk, and paints all ready for the operation. I knew well enough what Beauty's coming meant. It was only a prelude to my making a sketch of her; so I prepared with a good grace to receive all the hints which oozed out in due time. This occupied me the remainder of my mornings while I stayed at the Manor; and as the afternoons were devoted to driving and croquet, and the evenings to dancing and singing, I had no time to myself, but was kept in a continual whirl of occupation which had nothing to do with the many things I wanted to do. Poor Lady Garrington! she is kindness itself, and very warmhearted, but she does not realize the fact that people have their own interests and pursuits which they may wish to attend to. She has an idea that there cannot be any happiness in the world without some sort of gaiety; that the moment breakfast has been disposed of a *carte* must be arranged for the disposal of every hour of the day; and that a country house must be the abode of dulness unless one is always on the trot hunting after amusement and diversion of some kind. There never can be any repose where she is, and I am no longer surprised at the way in which Lord G—— shuts himself up in his own room and is scarcely visible except at meal-times. Yet her kindness is so great, and she has so much real desire to make her guests happy, and takes so much trouble to effect it (though it must be confessed that she likes to do it her own way and not theirs), that one cannot quarrel with her, or be otherwise than touched by her wish to make her house pleasant.' * * *

The remainder of Mrs. D——'s letter related to matters which concerned only herself and her son, and possess no interest for others. Her week at Garrington Manor is a fair sample of life at some country houses, where there are marriageable daughters, and where frantic efforts are being made for the amusement of the company. To those who are neither in their *première jeunesse* nor have daughters on hand, such a life is a positive penance, from which one is only too glad to escape in spite of all its hospitality.

VISITS IN COUNTRY HOUSES.

No. II.

WHEN Mrs. D—— and her son separated after the London season, each bent upon as full an enjoyment of country life as could be obtained, they made a compact to acquaint each other with their experiences. Mrs. D—— fulfilled her part of the contract in the letter which she wrote to her son Arthur from the Garringtons, in which she described very vividly one phase of society in country houses. Arthur's first visit was to one of his oldest friends, who was a millionaire and a large landed proprietor in the West of England. Sir Archibald Edmonstone had been Arthur's friend at Eton and at Oxford, and now it rarely happened that either of them went to Richmond, or Ascot, or Epsom, or, in fact, any party of pleasure in which the other was not his companion. Scarcely a day passed without their meeting either at their respective homes, or in Rotten Row, or at their clubs. No brothers were ever more inseparable; and the first move which Arthur made out of London was in the direction of Garzington Hall, where he was to pick up Sir Archibald and accompany him to Scotland.

Garzington Hall was a large modern house, situated in the midst of a fine old park which had belonged to the Edmonstones for generations. It was a place to be proud of, for it was very beautiful, surrounded by the most magnificent woods, and, from some points, commanding very fine views of the sea, which was about eight miles off as the crow flies. Sir Archibald was about a year older than his friend. His house was still the home of his brother and sisters, who did all they could to make it pleasant to their brother and his friends. He deserved this of them, for there never was a more dutiful son nor a kinder brother; and his great wish was that when he came of age there should be no change in the old ways. Often had his mother remonstrated, saying it was better for her to get out of the way betimes before his wife came to turn her out; to which remonstrance he invariably replied, 'Time enough, mother, time enough. I love my liberty too well to part with it just yet.'

The Edmonstone family consisted of three sisters and a younger brother, who was still at Eton. They were a racketting lot. Two of the sisters were 'out,' and the third and youngest on the very verge of that interesting moment in every young lady's life, when she bids adieu for ever to the school room and mixes in the gay and giddy world. They were rather 'fast,' and rather noisy; greater favourites with the gentlemen than with those of their own sex, who were somewhat afraid of them. They could ride well, and across country, too, sometimes; they could pull an oar across the lake which formed the southern boundary of the garden; they could skate, and had been known to shoot, and were not bad shots either. They were almost invincible at croquet; and the knack with which they sent their adversaries' ball flying across the ground was the envy of many of the gentlemen. They could play at billiards, too; and yet the more feminine accomplishments of singing and drawing had not been by any means neglected. Their mother, Lady Theodosia, was a very clever woman—rather blue, but decidedly clever and original, and with a horror of conventionalisms which prevented her seeing any objection to many of the amusements in which her daughters excelled, but for which many of her friends blamed her and them behind their backs, denouncing them as mannish, unladylike and noisy girls, and congratulating themselves and thanking Heaven and blessing their stars that *their* daughters had more regard for the conveniences of society and for what they called 'decorum.' But the Miss Edmonstones were as good, honest, warm-hearted, and generous girls as could be found, singularly free from the petty jealousies which disfigure so many of their own age and sex. Nor were they by any means devoid of talent; they inherited a fair share of their mother's cleverness, and could converse as pleasantly and rationally as most people and much more pleasantly than most girls of their age.

They were free from *mauvaise honte*, and yet by no means free and easy. Devoted to their brother, they were always ready for any fun of his suggesting, confident that he never would mislead them into doing anything that was really unbecoming, or could compromise them in the remotest degree. Such was the family by whom Arthur was always well received as one of their brother's oldest and best friends. At this time there was a large gathering for certain cricket matches which usually came off about this time. To make them a more popular institution in the neighbourhood, Lady Theodosia collected as many young people together as she could, and while the days were devoted to cricket, which was anxiously watched by crowds of neighbours and guests for whose accommodation marquees had been conveniently placed, the evenings were spent in tableaux and dancing, which left little time for repose, and made Garzington Hall the most popular place in the county. All the country belles looked forward to these annual gatherings and festivities as their 'red-letter days;' and as speculations upon them were the general theme of conversation before they took place, so their reminiscences were canvassed over and over again. It was from Garzington that Arthur's first letter was dated.

'MY DEAREST MOTHER,—You are wondering why I don't write, and have been abusing me like a pickpocket for my silence; but if you only knew what we have been doing day after day your wonder would turn altogether the other way. Even now I am writing at 4 A.M. with only one eye open, the other being fast asleep, for I am dead tired, and if I had any time to think about anything I dare say I should find out that I had every conceivable ache that over-fatigue can produce. But don't let your maternal heart become anxious on my account. I am very well, though nearly worn out with the endless racket of this place. Cricket by day and dancing by night leave one's legs very little time to rest. Luckily, Lady Theodosia is very merciful, and gives us some law at breakfast-time. I am generally the last, and, if I dared, would be later still, for, somehow, I am more tired when I get up than when I go to bed. At about 11.30 the wickets are pitched, and by 12 o'clock we are at work. The weather has been fine, and almost too hot. Unluckily, I have always been on the losing side, but we have had capital matches. You will care more for a description of the folk, their names, weights, and colours, than for any account of the matches, which are the engrossing subject here; and yet I think you will like to know the sort of life it is. There has been a cricket match every day, and as it generally lasts till dressing-time there is really very little time for anything else. Then dinner is succeeded by preparations for "tableaux," which are in their turn followed by dancing. I honestly confess that I think this is too much of a good thing. On one or two occasions, when the cricket was over sooner than usual, we were instantly had in request for croquet matches, in which the ladies certainly excelled. Theo. Edmonstone is the best croquet-player I ever saw. I wish you could have seen how well she put down that conceited young puppy Parker. It was as good as a play. You must know that "Happy Parker," as he is called, considers himself an awful swell. He is rich, rather good-looking, and has been, I am told, the spoilt child of fortune. He is in the blues, and is made a fuss with because he has lots of money, good horses, good shooting, and a good temper. He thinks the whole world is ready to be his humble servant. He had never been at Garzington before, and scarcely knows Edmonstone, never saw Lady Theodosia, and was once introduced to the second girl, Nina, who holds him in special aversion. I never saw any one so cool, free and easy, and off-hand as he is. He swaggers about as if he was bent on showing off his paces, and behaves as if he was the most intimate friend of the family instead of what he is, almost a stranger. One night, when Theo. Edmonstone had been looking after some of the guests, and had been getting partners for some of her country neighbours, and was standing alone and apart from the dancers, "Happy Parker" comes up with an air and a grace, and in a cool, off-hand way says to her, " You're doing nothing; would you like to dance with me? Come along." To which she quietly replied, looking him full in the face, "No I thank you; that would indeed be one degree worse than doing nothing." He looked awfully sold ; but he had found his match, for she is the last girl to stand any nonsense of that sort, and it is time for him to be brought to his bearings. You talk of not having a moment to yourself Like Miss Miggs, you consider you are always toiling, moiling, never "giving satisfaction, never having time to clean yourself—a potter's wessel ;" but what would you think of this life? It would kill the strongest man in no time at all, and would flog Banting out of the field. You are hunted from cricket to croquet, from croquet to tableaux and charades, and then to dancing, and the intervening time is devoted to dressing and dining, and you are lucky if you get to bed by 4 o'clock A.M.; for, after the ball, we men adjourn to the smoking-room, where we wind up the festivities with cigars and cooling beverages, and talk over the events of the day, and criticise some fair *débutante* who has blossomed for the first time at the Garrington Ball. To-night, the last of the series, we wound up with Sir Roger de Coverley, sang God save the Queen and Jolly Dogs all in chorus, and gave sundry cheers for Lady Theodosia and the house of Edmonstone.

'But now about the "other folk." The house has been as full as it can hold, and several men sleep over the stables, your humble servant among the number. Lord and Lady Camelford and their son and daughter, Lady Blanche Ross and her husband, Lady Georgina Roach and her two daughters, besides the Thompsons, those very pretty Miss Nashes, and Lord and Lady Fairlight, and some country neighbours. There are, of course, a lot of men, "loose men" as Lady —— would call them, some of whom are invited because of their skill at cricket. Tom Lee and young Drystix are among the number. As usual, Tom Lee is the autocrat of the cricket-field, the ball-room, and smoking-room. He lays down the law in the most insufferable manner, and considers no one has any right to do anything of any kind without his permission. I cannot imagine why he is asked everywhere, for very few people like him, as his cool indifference with regard to the likes and dislikes of his neighbours almost amounts to impertinence. His success last year when he was on the Northern Circuit has made him more unbearable than ever. But as he is too unpleasant a subject to dwell upon, I will tell you about the tableaux. Lady Fairlight and the youngest of the three Miss Nashes were the belles. You cannot imagine anything more beautiful than Lady Fairlight as Mary Queen of Scots at her execution. Lady Camelford's daughter and the Miss Roaches were her maids of honour, and young Lord Tufton was the executioner. Lady Fairlight was dressed in black velvet. In the first tableau she appeared absorbed in prayer while her maids of honour stood weeping around her; and in the second she was in the act of giving her "beads" to one of her ladies. I never saw anything like her expression in this last scene. It was a combination of resignation at her own sad fate and tender compassion for those she was about to leave for ever. The next tableau was from the "Rape of the Lock," in which the youngest of the Nashes represented Belinda. She was exquisitely dressed, and as her forehead is low the effect of her hair being drawn off away from her face was exceedingly good, especially as she has a good brow. Altogether with powder, and flowers jauntily set on the top and side of the mountain of coiffure which she wore, and with patches, and sac, and short petticoats displaying a small foot and neat ankle, she was as lovely a sight as could be seen. Tom Lee did his part well. His unwhiskered face came in admirably for such a tableau. He was capitally dressed, and so were Miss Nash's two sisters, who filled up the background. The last tableau was of Elaine as she was borne along in her barge. Ellen Pendarve's fine outline came out beautifully as she lay upon the bier, and Lord Camelford's masculine head and features with the addition of a snowy beard well represented the "dumb old servitor" who steer'd the dead "upward with the flood."

' In her right hand the lily, in her left
The letter—all her bright hair streaming down—
And all the coverlid was cloth of gold
Down to her waist, and she herself in white
All but her face, and that clear-featured face
Was lovely, for she did not seem as dead
But fast asleep, and lay as though she smiled.'

I am not sure it was wise to finish the tableaux with one so sad—for it was not easy to shake off the impression quickly, and it was only by a kind of an effort that we returned to jollity. However, we did manage to recover ourselves, and were as jolly as ever, dancing away merrily to fiddle and fife. Our charades were even better than the tableaux; and some of the acting was admirable. Young Drystix made a first-rate conspirator in "Counterplot," and Lord Tufton a capital man milliner. The passages between him and Theo. Edmonstone were admirable. "The Peer," as Tom Lee, his bear leader, calls him, has a quantity of black, greasy-looking hair, a bright colour, good features, and an incipient moustache, which he is always manipulating tenderly; and altogether he well represented that peculiar class of mankind which is devoted to measuring tapes and laces by the yard and to proffering their goods to the fair sex in the most irresistible manner. It seemed to me quite his *métier* to unfold silks and satins, and assure the purchasers that they were "the newest style," the "most fashionable," "quite distinguished," &c., &c. Theo. Edmonstone's contemptuous banter of him, and reckless inconsiderateness in making him display his goods, without the remotest intention of purchasing any, exhibited to the life the mode in which some ladies of our acquaintance conduct themselves in certain shops which profess to provide them with all that is requisite to their success and reputation in society. And now, dear mother mine, I must shut up and get to bed, for Edmonstone and I are off early to-morrow on our way to the North. I will write to you again as soon as I can, but if we are worked as hard at Stapleton's as we have been here, I shall not have much time to write. What a pity and a bore too, it is that some of the kindest-hearted and most good-natured people in the world make life such a toil to themselves and their friends. There are people who are always striving to get fourteen pence out of every shilling, and so there are others whose sole object is to get more hours out of every day than is to be got, and so it is all "hurry scurry" after amusement of some kind.'

Arthur and Sir Archibald set off early, and travelled as luxuriously and comfortably together as it is possible in this most luxurious age. By dint of proper precautions, in direct contravention of the orders and regulations issued by the directors, and in contempt of the penalties and anathemas annexed to any infringement of those orders, the two friends were able to propitiate the guards so as to secure for themselves the undisputed and undisturbed possession of one compartment, in which they slept and smoked and talked and read as they felt inclined; and in due course of time they arrived at their destination, where they had been invited for grouse-shooting and deer-stalking. The nickname by which 'the Lodge' was known among a certain set of familiar friends was 'Liberty Hall,' because the owner and master of it piqued himself upon allowing every one to do just what he liked, and neither more nor less than he pleased. The bee might be as busy as he would, and the drone as idle. It was from Liberty Hall that Arthur despatched his second letter to his mother.

'DEAREST MOTHER,—It seems to me the world is always in extremes. At Garzington we were never allowed a moment to ourselves. We were hunted from pillar to post, never might be sulky or indulge any wayward fancy of one's own; and here we are allowed to do what we like, go where we like, and indulge any passing mood. I have been here a week, and have very little to tell you; but you will rail at me, and return to your old charge against all men, and say that they can never be pleased, if I say that I do not think the absence of all rule and law, as it exists at "Liberty Hall," conduces to one's comfort. The fact is, than when the master of the house surrenders his right to plan and devise for the amusement of his guests, every one is at a loss to know what to do, and the practical result is that we either go about amusing ourselves in a "shilly-shally" kind of way, or else submit to the dictation of some ruling but less scrupulous individual who forces his own views upon others as to what is or is not the thing to be done. We have at this moment an instance in point. Hervey Gray, a cousin of our host, presumes upon his relationship, and absorbs all the "gillies," and directs us all with much more imperiousness than his cousin ever would assume. At the beginning of our visit we were left very much to ourselves, and had each of us a gilly of our own, and whatever else we wanted, but there was no plan—no combination,—and it did not answer, especially as the master of "Liberty Hall" is not himself much of a sportsman, and has taken "the Lodge" more for the honour and glory of the thing than for his own special love of sport; but now Hervey Gray rules us with a rod of iron, and, though fond of shooting, but very ignorant of the noble art of deer-stalking, lays down the law for us, for the keepers, for the gillies, for everybody and everything, and his law is not always good or pleasant. In short, I am altogether rather out of humour, and think that it is possible to have too much of one's own way, and that Hervey

Gray is not a good substitute for the laird of "Liberty Hall."

'Arthur D—— was quite right in saying that it does not conduce to comfort when the master is not master. It is like an arch without its keystone; there is no centre, no point of union. The combination of law and liberty is rare, but where it exists, it promotes happiness. It sounds almost absurd to use such grand words and ideas for the expression of a very simple fact—that the pleasantest houses are those in which the owners occupy themselves for the comfort and entertainment of their guests, and arrange for them what shall be done, and at the same time make it quite appreciable by all that each one is at liberty to say "yea" or "nay" according to the bias of his own mind. It is difficult to steer clear of the two opposite evils of which Garzington Manor and Liberty Hall are the types; but there are houses in which the gifted hosts and hostesses contrive to provide for their guests whatever shall be most conducive to their enjoyment without fussiness or dictation. No one is neglected; all are considered; and life passes so easily and pleasantly, without noise or confusion, that we thinking people are scarcely conscious of the amount of tact, consideration, and forethought which they ought to place to the credit of those who make it a part of the business of their life to contribute, as far as they can, to the social enjoyment of their friends.

'TOM SLENDER.'

VISITS IN COUNTRY HOUSES.

No. III.

AFTER having mutually followed their own devices, Mrs. D—— and her son Arthur agreed to meet at Hornby Castle, where the Duke of Broadlands entertained a large party, to celebrate the coming of age of his eldest son, Lord Proudacre.

Hornby Castle well represented the family to whom it had belonged for so many years. It was a stately, turreted castle, which had been built about a century ago, on the site of an old house which, for many generations, had satisfied the more moderate requirements of those who were then lords of the manor of Hornby; for 'Hornby Manor' had not then developed into 'Hornby Castle.' It was left to after generations to form alliances, and accumulate wealth and land, which placed the Duke of Broadlands on a level with the most noble and wealthy. By a marriage with the greatest heiress of her day, and the sole representative of an ancient house, whose alliance had been universally courted for many preceding generations, they took the name of 'Goldust;' and after adding field to field, and enlarging their borders, they pulled down the old house, which had sheltered them and theirs with its ancient respectability for so long a time, and whose walls had resounded with the merry voices of all the children who had grown up under its roof, and built a gorgeous castle, which, as we have already said, well represented the estate of its noble occupiers. It was a handsome building, if turrets and towers, and a huge mass of masonry, covering a considerable area, constitute beauty of any kind. All who appreciate what is genuine, and hate pretension, turned away from it, if not with disgust, at all events with dissatisfaction at there being so little to interest them. It was impossible to help being attracted by its immensity. It overawed the beholder as it stretched itself out along the valley, occupying, with its stables and outbuildings, which were all built in the same massive and imposing style, with its gardens, and lawns, and pleasure-grounds, a vast extent of land, infinitely greater than any one would suppose from merely looking down upon it from the heights above. Nature had proved herself a kind friend to Hornby Castle, for nothing could surpass the beauty of the park and its surrounding scenery. Wood and water, fern, heather, and gorse, undulating ground, well-wooded hills protecting it from the cruel north winds; and on the southern side an extensive view over a rich and beautifully-wooded country, which melted away into the blue distance of the far horizon. Such a prospect could rarely be seen, and many an eye rested on it in silent pleasure, glad to turn away from the castle itself, which afforded so little interest. All that wealth could accomplish had been done to adorn the castle. Inside and out it told of money, but, great and imposing as it was, it sunk into less than insignificance in the presence of Nature.

Hornby Castle now appeared in its most attractive form; for so large a house, filled as it was throughout, from top to bottom, and in every nook, with a goodly assemblage of persons of all ages, bent upon enjoying themselves, and doing all possible honour to the occasion which called them together, could not fail in affording amusement and pleasure to its guests. It was so large that, when fully inhabited, it seemed almost to contain the population of a small town; and this circumstance in itself was a security for success, because every one was sure to find some congenial society. The young are easily pleased, and ready to find some good in everything. To them every cloud has a silver lining; and nothing is wholly evil in their eyes. But their elders are neither so easily satisfied nor so well disposed.

They are more critical, and more *exigéant*—more something which interferes with their enjoyment of life. But at Hornby Castle he must have been very crabbed and hard to please who could not find something pleasant and congenial in the varied society which was now collected in honour of Lord Proudacre's having attained his majority. Mothers with lovely daughters—and of course all mothers think their daughters lovely—were in a flutter of delight, for who could tell that the young millionaire might not be *épris* with one of them? At all events, it was not impossible, and, to many minds, what is not absolutely impossible soon becomes hopeful. It had been a profitable time for the milliners, for no expense was spared by the 'chaperons' to embellish the appearance of their lovely charges. Everything that could set off their wares to the best advantage on so important an occasion was universally voted to be money well spent, which might, possibly, return a high interest. There was that vulgar Lady Chesterford with her daughter, no longer young, but who imagined she possessed the gift of eternal youth, and who always selected the last and most popular *débutante* as her 'dear friend,' as if all the rest were too old to be her companions. She was always, like her mother, dressed in the most *outré* fashion; and it was said, and generally believed, that poor Lord Chesterford, who had nothing but his pension as a retired and now superannuated chancellor, found himself nearly swamped by the costliness and variety of the *toilettes* of his wife and daughter. He was a somewhat prosy man, but could tell a story well; and his everlasting reminiscences obtained for him a certain amount of success. He was one of the Duke of Broadlands' oldest political friends, and they used to retire into remote corners to settle the affairs of the state, which, if the expression of their faces, and the solemnity of their manner might be taken as any indication of its condition, it might be inferred that the country was on the very verge of ruin. Then there was Lady Caroline Hardy and her daughter, who is one of the beauties of the day, but who, for some inexplicable reason, is not popular. Whether she is dull or ill-tempered it is impossible to say, because opinion is divided, but she has not the success to which her beauty entitles her. Her mother was a celebrated beauty, but not overwise; and it was always said that her husband was not sorry to die, and used to say, with a *double entendre* in his words, that he had prayed for many years for his release. Mr. and Lady Barbara Bucket and their son and daughter contributed their share to the entertainment of the company at Hornby Castle. She was an ambitious woman, who was always aiming at being the *grande dame* of the county in which she lived. She was a discreet woman, for she never let any one know the inside of her mind. It was possible it had no inside; but if it had she guarded it well, so that no one should look into it. She had an eternal smile, of a peculiar kind, in which the thin upper lip seemed lost in teeth; and say what you would, of sorrow or joy, you were sure to be greeted by the same inexpressive smile. Her sole object in life was to become the reigning queen of Swampshire. Her husband was a man who lived upon the news he gleaned from other men, and he had a peculiar way of creeping up to people who were engaged in conversation, that he might learn the subject of it. His thirst for information was unbounded, and he was generally known as 'the Swampshire Investigator.' He would have made an admirable reporter had his lot in life been cast differently. As it was, he was always welcomed by those who live upon other people's affairs, and room was always made for him in certain coteries of tea-drinking elderly women, who invariably greeted him by saying, 'Ah, here's Mr. Bucket; he is sure to know all about it. He will tell us. Oh, Mr. Bucket, we are so glad to see you. Have you heard whether it is true that Lady Jones called her husband Sir Henry an old fool, because he lost thirty shillings at whist to Sir Ralph Gambler? And do you know whether it is true that Lord and Lady Goosey are going to be separated because they are already tired of each other? You are sure to know, because you know everything.' Then Mr. Bucket would twiddle his watch-key, and would say that he 'did not know, but had heard,' &c. All these people furnished a fund of amusement to those who appreciated their propensities, or liked to play them off for the entertainment of others.

Mrs. D—— and her son were such pleasant, cheery, and unpretentious people that they were always well received; besides which they were so pleasant to themselves and one another, that they were, without any effort on their part, agreeable company generally. Mrs. D——, who had a natural gift for private theatricals, was in great request; and as she loved burnt cork, footlights, and everything connected with the stage, she was in her element at once, ready to give a helping hand wherever it was wanted. She could improvise a dress out of very scanty materials, and could compose the most successful prologue on the shortest notice. She could arrange a tableau with true artistic skill; and as tableaux and private theatricals were a part of the programme of the festivities, she was in hourly requisition—the referee on all disputed points, who could, with her consummate tact, make people do exactly what they were required to do. She and her son Arthur, in the meanwhile, entertained themselves each day by comparing notes, and commenting on the events as they occurred; and the daily reunions between mother and son were the best commentary of the proceedings which took place on the momentous occasion of Lord Proudacre's attaining his majority.

Not only in the immediate neighbourhood of Hornby Castle, but throughout the length and breadth of the county of Tuftunshire the Duke of Broadlands was held in great awe and respect. His word was law; his disapproval a grave calamity. Surrounded by small squires and self-important clergy, he reigned like a king over the whole county; and they who were so fortunate as to be admitted within the gracious precincts of Hornby Castle, and into the Duke's confidence, were the envy of all their neighbours, and themselves elated at the notice that was taken of them. It was quite a tradition in the county that the mind of his Grace, on all local politics, should be taken before any one would venture to move in any matter; and when, on a certain memorable occasion, one of the squires of Tuftunshire presumed to have an opinion of his own, and to endeavour to maintain it against the Duke of Broadlands, the whole of that deferential county was aghast at his presumption, and was in haste to propitiate the favour of the Duke, and assure him that it was but an isolated instance of a man daring to think for himself. The clergy and the gentry were, in fact, more or less dependents of the great man. They who were in favour were flattered by it to their very bent, and they who were not lived on hoping, even against hope, that their turn might come some day. The submissiveness and deference of these good people, their anxiety to propitiate the rising sun, and to do all honour to the Goldust family, was a source of great amusement to Mrs. D—— and her son, who commented on the flunkeyism of these country folk in no measured terms.

'Mother,' said Arthur D—— one day, as he sat in Mrs. D——'s room, in the interval before dressing-time, talking over the events of the day, and canvassing the various guests who had arrived,—'Mother, did you see what a fix that poor Mr. Luvtin was in when the "great man" called on him to repeat what he was saying to that young liberal, Harry Phreethink? How he stammered and spluttered; and how sold he was when Harry, enjoying the fun, said that Mr. Luvtin was agreeing with him in thinking that there should be an extension of the franchise, but that they had only as yet agreed that a bill should be introduced, but had not settled the details.'

'Oh! that was it, then, that made the Duke give one of his ominous "Ah's!"'

'Yes; and did you see how it shut up poor old Luvtin? I pitied the man. He won't sleep a wink while he is in the house, because he will feel he has regularly put his foot into it. How I did enjoy it, though!'

'It was a shame, though, my dear Arthur, of your friend Harry to make so much mischief.'

'Mischief, mother! why, bless you, it will blow over in no time.'

'Never, Arthur. The Duke never allows the clergy to think for themselves. Besides, if I mistake not, Mr. Luvtin has one of the Duke's livings.'

Arthur gave no reply, save a prolonged whistle.

'What are you going to do, mother, about that young Raffles? He'll never know his part, and he is such an awful stick. In that love scene with Eva Robarts (by Jove, mother, what a pretty girl she is!) he provokes me out of all patience.'

'No doubt, my boy; I can well believe it. Would you like to take his place?'

'Nonsense! I don't mean that. I am not such a fool as that. Why, the girl has not a penny, mother.'

'I admire your philosophy, Arthur; and, after all, "her face is her fortune," as the old song says.'

'I want to ask you, mother, who is that Doctor Medlar, that seems to be such an authority in arranging some of the tableaux?'

'I cannot tell, except that he is a great friend of the Duchess's—her own pet doctor that she swears by, and who seems to have the run of the house.'

'I hate the man!'

'So do I.'

'Did you see how he took hold of Emily Fitzgibbon's chin, and said, "A little more this way, if you please—a *leetle* more still. Thank you; that will do. Now the head a little thrown back; thank you. Allow me," and again the fellow took hold of her chin to arrange her *pose* as he liked. I had no patience with him.'

'And how did Emily Fitzgibbon like it?'

'Like it! She looked as if she could have knocked him down. Did you hear that after it was over she went up to Lady Lavinia Goldust, and said she must decline taking any further part in the tableaux?'

'No; did she though! I wonder whether that is really true, because Lord Proudacre seems rather taken with her, and I don't somehow think she would like to affront them.'

'Perhaps not; but I can tell you she was awfully put out; and when that little doctor came forward afterwards, to assure her that it was the best tableau of the evening, she scarcely vouchsafed him any reply, but gave him a look expressive of ineffable contempt. I think it was, after all, your fault, mother.'

'Mine! How could it be mine? What could I have to do with that man?'

'You could have prevented his interfering.'

'Lady Lavinia and her mother assigned to us our proper places, and, as you know, I am mistress of the robes, and have to arrange all about the dresses. I am the genius that presides over calico, cotton, velvet, and the rouge-pot. But there goes the dressing-bell, and if you don't hurry off I shall not be in time for dinner, and shall again offend against the laws of Hornby Castle, of which punctuality is one.'

'I say, mother, what a pompous, stiff old prig he is.'

'Yes; but a most kindhearted man. I have known him do the most generous acts, in spite of his character for stint and screw.'

'Well, I must be off, else I shall offend his mightiness.'

Every day they sat down fifty to dinner. There was a magnificent state dining-room, capable of accommodating a vast number, and even this large party was not out of proportion to it. It was built of stone, with richly groined roof, and handsome oak panelling occupied one-third of the walls. A huge fireplace and richly-carved stone chimney-piece filled up the centre of the room, reaching almost up to the ceiling; while a large oriel window opposite the fireplace, and another of the same character, only larger still, at right angles to it, added to its appearance. It was one of those rooms which strike the beholder with awe. It required numbers to be able to grapple with its oppressive magnificence, and a smaller party would have been silenced by it. As it was, the room resounded with the sound of merry voices, and there was no lull in the laughter and merriment that prevailed. The first day the Duke of Broadlands seemed bewildered by the unwonted sounds, and, had he dared, would have been tempted to read the Riot Act; but his astonishment gave way before the resolute determination of every one to enjoy himself, and he was carried away by the strong current, and found himself at last taking part in the surrounding revelry.

As the Duchess left the dining-room, she went up to the Duke and begged him not to remain there long, as so much had to be done in the way of entertainment for the large company of neighbours who were expected to arrive for the tableaux and ball which was to succeed them.

The tenantry had been already regaled in the most sumptuous manner. The preceding day, which was the important one in Lord Proudacre's life, had been devoted to feasting the tenants and the poor on the estate. Each poor family had beef and bread, plum-pudding and beer, and a week's wages; and every cottage bore ample testimony to the unwonted generosity and liberality of the Duke of Broadlands. The tenants had been assembled in a large iron room which had been erected for the occasion, and all the company at the Castle dined with them, and it was generally voted to have been great fun. The Duke relaxed somewhat from his wonted dignity of manner, and actually condescended to some playful witticisms in his intercourse with his tenants. Lord Proudacre acquitted himself more than creditably; and there were some who were malicious enough to say that there were indications of his views becoming more liberal than any which had hitherto prevailed at Hornby Castle—a suspicion which never entered the Duke's head, happily both for himself and Lord Proudacre; for if such an idea had suggested itself to him as a possibility, it must have led to distrust and estrangement, as the Duke looked upon political consistency as the greatest of moral virtues, and would have preferred any *esclandre* to the abandonment of the family tradition.

No sooner had the gentlemen left the dining-room, than Mrs. D—— was hurried off to her green-room, where, with rouge-pot, paint, and powder, she was soon busily employed in putting the finishing touches to those who were to figure in the tableaux. Dr. Medlar was busy on the stage, in front of which a large gold frame was fastened, across the inside of which some crape had been strained. But the little doctor was the presiding genius, giving offence to all save the Duchess, who could see no fault in her 'dear Doctor Medlar.' He was a little man, with bright eyes, a hook-nose, and brilliant complexion; not unlike a Jew, very unlike a gentleman, with effeminate, would-be-insinuating manners. Mrs. D—— was referred to very often, because the spirit of rebellion against the doctor was very general, and none of the ladies, young or old, liked to be twisted and twirled about at his pleasure, as if they were nothing better than lay figures.

There was the scene between Jeanie and Effie Deans in prison; between Sir Henry Lee and Alice, where she kneels at his feet, while he sat in a wicker arm-chair, listening to a respectable old man whose dilapidated dress showed something of the clerical habit; and another in which the Fair Maid of Perth listens, in an attitude of devout attention, to the instructions of a Carthusian monk. But one of the happiest of all was a Dutch picture, in which a family group was represented, some engaged in needlework, others playing at cards, while some younger ones played with their toys on the floor, as their elders slept soundly in their armchairs, with half-emptied glasses by their side. The grouping, the varied dresses, all the accessories told so well that it took every one by surprise, and elicited the most enthusiastic applause. After these were over, they adjourned to the drawing-rooms, and then reassembled in the saloon, where dancing was kept up until a late hour.

The next morning, Arthur D—— felt disinclined to join the party in the racket-court, and, yawning from sheer fatigue (for he had been in great request for the tableaux, and was an inveterate dancer), he sauntered leisurely into his mother's room, saying —

'Well, mother, will you bet? Is Proudacre going to marry Emily Fitzgibbon?'

'Marry Emily Fitzgibbon!—not he. Why, no Goldust ever married a Whig. The Duke would die of it.'

'But, mother, fellows sometimes think for themselves on such matters.'

'Perhaps so: but that will never be. I should pity her if it were to take place, for she would not have a comfortable berth of it.'

'Why so?'

'Because the Duke takes upon himself the responsibility of thinking for all his family, and he would never forgive the intrusion of such thorough Whig blood into his house.'

'Is he such a bigot in politics?'

'Yes, indeed; in politics, in religion, in everything. Don't you see in what awe he is held by all the county-people?—how they bow and scrape when they come within a hundred yards of him?'

'By-the-by, did you see what a fright young Snobere was in, when he nearly knocked his Grace over as he was waltzing with that gay Mrs. Neerdowell? He stammered his apologies as if his last hope of heaven was on the very verge of being lost. He was in such an awful fright.'

'Who is it you are speaking of, Arthur? Is it that round, chubby-faced youth who asked you, when you were in the green-room, what sort of tap they kept at Hornby Castle?'

'Yes, mother, the same. He was the fellow you padded so nicely for the sleepy Dutchman in the "Family Group."'

'I remember; and who has been making such violent love to Blanche Oxenford.'

'Exactly; whenever, at least, Mrs. Neerdowell will let him.'

'By-the-by, Arthur, who is that Mrs. Neerdowell? She is very pretty; but rather dangerous, isn't she?'

'Well, there are all sorts of stories about her. Some say she is a widow; others that she is a *divorcée*'

'What? a *divorcée* at Hornby Castle! Why, the very walls would fall upon us if such a thing were even suspected. But what is she?'

'I cannot tell: I have been trying to find out. She came with those Merewothers that the Duke was so civil to.'

'And she is determined to take our fat Dutchman by storm; and he, foolish fellow! is flattered by it. Arthur, you men are silly fellows.'

'Because, dear mother, you women are so pleasant. Isn't that it?'

'I don't know why it is; only that there is no man that a clever woman cannot make a fool of. You remember Samson?'

Arthur looked grave, and then asked his mother when she intended to leave Hornby Castle.

'I am rather tired of all this row. Cannot we take a small cottage somewhere, and rusticate a little while? I don't care where it is. We might get down some books from Mudie's, and read and be quiet; for it seems to me that, wherever one visits in the country, one is sure to find as much row and racket as there is in London, with fewer opportunities of escaping from it and of doing what one likes.'

'But, my dear Arthur, you are quite *blasé*. What does it all mean? You did not suppose that, when we came here for this special occasion, we should find the house empty, or do nothing but twiddle finger and thumb from morning to night. 1

was here once, some years ago, when there was scarcely any one here but ourselves, and I never shall forget the pompous solemnity of it all. Oh, no! take my word for it that Hornby Castle is only bearable when there is what you call a "row" going on.'

'Ah, my dear mother, you are so fond of society.'

'Fond of my own kind? Yes, and so will you be when you are as old as I am. It is only the young who think it a happiness to sit at home and live upon themselves.'

'Not at all: I do not wish for that. But just remember where we have been. You found row and racket at the Garringtons; I found the same at Garzington. And then at Filey with the Splashfords, and at Danesford with the Neverests; and now here there is not a moment's quiet. Morning, noon, and night the top is made to spin.'

'But you were not any more contented with your life in the Highlands.'

'No; but that was for a different reason: because there was no guiding hand to direct and arrange what was to be done.'

'My dear boy, you are, like the rest of your sex, never contented.'

'Indeed, no. I am not discontented; but I own that I like to sit here with you, and——'

'Grumble.'

'No, mother; you are wrong.'

'What, then, do you call it? and why should you be so weary? I can remember when you never could have enough of it; when I had to run after Lady This, and Mrs. That, to get invitations for you, and spent a fortune in note-paper to get you into all the row and racket you now profess to dislike.'

'Well, mother, it was so; and I suppose that I have had enough of it. "All work, and no play, makes Jack a dull boy;" but I suspect, all play would make him very sick. But tell me—was it like this in your day, when you were quite young?'

'I am amused at the delicate way in which you say *quite* young, as if you wished to let me down easy. No; things were very different in my young days. We used to pay longer visits than are now paid, and visited at fewer houses. Travelling was a more difficult and expensive affair. We had more friends and fewer acquaintances then. Now the tables are turned, and friendships are comparatively rare. It is all owing to the facility of travelling, which has made us more restless, and more dependent upon excitement.'

Mrs. D—— was not far wrong. Steam has set society in motion; and go where we will, we find everything in a state of progress. It is only in such places as Hornby Castle, weighted as it is by the pompous old Duke of Broadlands, that things seem to stand still; and yet even there, as we have lately seen, circumstances have proved too strong for him; and Hornby Castle will live in Arthur D——'s memory as a place in which there was as little quiet as could be found in other places which are avowedly given up to pleasure.

WHAT'S IN THE PAPERS?

(ILLUSTRATED BY THE LATE C. H. BENNETT.)

WELL, as far as matters of intense personal interest are concerned, it entirely depends upon your own peculiar hobby; but, if you are merely anxious to learn the contents of 'The Times,' 'Daily Telegraph,' 'Standard,' or 'Morning Star,' as a matter of statistics in journalism, I can sum them up and give you the result in a twinkling. Leading articles, reports, critiques; intelligence on military, naval, sporting, and mercantile matters; foreign correspondence, advertisements, and pudding. If you can find nothing whatever to amuse you in any of these departments, you may just as well give up the study of newspapers for ever, and stick to the perusal of fiction for the remainder of your days. I am fully convinced, for my own part, that a belief in reality is fatal to the exercise of the fancy: I only put my faith in things that cannot by any possibility be proved, and I am consequently looked upon (by people who don't know any better) as an ethereal dreamer—a creature of wild imaginings—a being of infinite aspirations; as anything, in short, rather than a practical and well-conducted young person. It is not, however, the wish of most people to imitate Lord Byron, and wear an enormous amount of back hair. The present age believes in its own doings considerably, and likes to see how it gets along; hence the enormous demand for newspapers.

I always make a point of reading my own particular organ of opinion in bed; and, having perused it through and through very carefully, I throw it down and give myself up to a luxurious criticism on all that it contains. Facts are not much in my line, as I have already stated; but Society demands that one should know something of what goes on in the world; and I desire to keep well with Society. To-night, perhaps—during the intervals of the mazy waltz or the maddening galop—I shall find myself in want of a subject on which to breathe soft nothings to my delightful partner. I shall probably dine this evening in the most intellectual company, and I wish to be particularly terse and epigrammatic on current events. The newspaper obviously supplies me with materials for the exhibition of my conversational acquirements; and I am enabled, by perusing it in bed, fully to digest its varied contents. The body's repose is propitious to the mind's exertion; and I have long ago discovered that my brain is never so active as when reclining on my downy pillow. Try to read a paper during breakfast, in the train, or on the omnibus: you cannot concentrate your intellect upon the task. It is merely one duty amongst the many that you have to perform during the day. Peruse it in bed, and it becomes your sole occupation—the only interval between rest and labour,—the neutral ground that separates dreaming from doing. Never tell me that you cannot afford the time for it. Let the servant wake you half an hour before you mean to rise.

The readers of a newspaper are as various in their choice of topics as the topics themselves. Nothing is too heavy for some of them, and nothing too light for others. There are people in this world, I believe, who take a fervid interest in the precise time of high water at London Bridge; yet high water and low are matters of profound indifference to most of us. The general reader cares very little about ships that have arrived and ships that have sailed; yet the departure o every ship makes a good many people very anxious, and the arrival of every ship makes a good many people very happy. The advertisements that begin with 'Wanted' have never created much interest in the bosom of your humble servant; yet they are devoured with considerable eagerness by poor folks out of employment. It is not at all

Drawn by the late C. H. Bennett.

WHAT'S IN THE PAPERS?

a common thing for the reader of a newspaper to occupy the centre of indifference on *every* subject contained in it. We all profess to entertain strong opinions on the question of politics now-a-days; and those who cultivate the most moderate principles appear to be the most outrageous in their talk. I always fight extremely shy of a man who tells me that he is a Liberal-Conservative, because I feel certain that he intends to get upon his hind legs and argue. He reminds me of Mr. Facing-both-ways, in the 'Pilgrim's Progress.' I like a stanch Conservative, and I love an enthusiastic Liberal. Only let a man be black or white; this whitey-brown school of politics is more than I can bear. The number of respectable householders in London who firmly believe that the British Empire would go to smithereens unless they had frequent opportunities of stating their private impressions respecting its government must be something absolutely enormous. They deliver themselves of their pet theories on all possible occasions, and very often learn a considerable portion of the previous night's Parliamentary debates by heart. The conduct of Lord Stanley in the 'Tornado' business, and the behaviour of Mr. Walpole respecting the demonstration in Hyde Park, must have set folks disputing in very nearly every coffee-room and eating-house in town. The newspaper student who reads politics for their own sake, generally contrives to make himself thoroughly master of his facts. His deductions, I need scarcely tell you, are occasionally erroneous; but the opponent who rashly attempts to confute his logic is generally suffering from a loose screw in his own statements. When one party in an argument can only *remember*, and the other can only *reason*, a considerable amount of precious time is likely to be lost in talk.

The gentleman who pays the Fine Arts the graceful compliment of cultivating about a couple of them to a modest extent, gives his first glance to the critiques. The Royal Academy, and the French and Flemish Exhibition are absorbing topics for him; he is quite capable of forming his own opinion on pictures, but he is nevertheless rather anxious to discover what the verdict of a professional critic may happen to be. He likes to find himself supported by authority, and so he studies the daily papers as well as the weekly reviews. He welcomes with joy the latest news regarding operas and concerts. The notices of new plays have a singular fascination for him, whether he believes or not in the decline of the drama. It gives him huge gratification to be told that Miss T. performed with her usual tenderness and grace in the three-act comedy produced somewhere last night, or that Miss F. was the life and soul of Mr. Somebody's latest burlesque. He is perhaps acquainted personally with a popular actor—in which case he possesses a strong qualification for becoming a consummate bore, both amongst those who are acquainted with *several* popular actors, and amongst those who are acquainted with none at all. Whenever his friend happens to be spoken well of in the papers he announces the fact with immense triumph in every circle that he pervades, to the unbounded joy of his listeners. He succeeds now and then in picking up very small pieces of green-room gossip. A certain actress is going to be married; or a certain actor appears before the public under an assumed name (his proper one being Smith or Jones, probably); and these infinitesimal scandals are whispered about with every demonstration of profound sagacity, until their garrulous chronicler has gradually come to be looked upon by the weak-minded as an oracle in dramatic affairs. His interest in the papers is greatly heightened by his knowledge of the names of the critics. If you are ever unlucky enough to go to the theatre in his company on the first night of a new piece, he will point you out 'The Times,' 'Telegraph,' and 'Star,' very knowingly.

The mercantile gentleman turns at once to the money article of his favourite organ. He is an eminently practical man, sir, and has been occupied during several years of his life in trying to spell some pretty word out of the three letters L, S, and D. He reads his paper in an omnibus or a railway carriage (first class) on his way to his place of business. The E.C. postal district is to him a garden in which he gathers money all the day, like a busy bee. Politics interest him inasmuch as they influence the funds. He is at present a Conservative, if anything: in the days of his clerkship, a long time ago, his tendency was towards the most pronounced Radicalism. On seventy or eighty pounds per annum, one *must* be a Radical, you see; Conservative principles cannot be nourished at the price. Except the City intelligence, there is very little in the paper to amuse our commercial friend; but he glances at the police reports when he gets to his chop-house, in the middle of the day, because reading is favourable to the process of digestion. He likes to hear about fraudulent bankrupts; and a good big forgery is meat and drink to him for several days.

To the lounger, *pur et simple*, the most seductive portion of a daily paper is its *padding*. This is the technical word made use of to describe those little scraps of general information, and odds and ends which are introduced at the foot of a column in order to fill it up. They are almost endless in their variety; and some such headings as the following may generally be looked for amongst them:—

Singular Discovery of Human Remains in a Chalk Pit.
The Bombay Mails.
Daring Robbery in the South of France.
Progress of the Metropolitan Improvements.
Fatal Termination to a Practical Joke.
Remarkable Atmospheric Phenomenon in Devonshire.

These entertaining morsels very often go the round of the London papers, and end by going out starring in the provinces. They are exceedingly useful as topics for small-talk; and I should advise all diners-out who feel their intellects insufficient for grappling with questions of importance to devote a considerable quantity of their spare time to the study of padding. Plenty of amusement can also be obtained from the perusal of those mysterious advertisements which entreat somebody to return to his disconsolate wife, or treat of 'an elderly man who left his home last week in a blue coat with brass buttons, a wide-awake hat, and a pair of patent-leather boots He was last seen at the British Museum, and is supposed to be insane.' It is interesting, too, to know that 'X received the 5*l.*, and will be happy to hear from Z again;' or that some incurable maniac has been sending money to the Chancellor of the Exchequer on account of unpaid income-tax. The cynic will find food for conversation in the announcement headed, 'Wanted a Governess.' The immense prices given for education just now are amongst the most encouraging signs of the times.

But it is quite impossible to exhaust the types of people who take delight in the newspaper — from the Minister of the Crown who is anxious to see whether his oration of last night in Parliament is correctly reported, to the sympathetic burglar who desires to know how his bosom friend conducted himself yesterday before the Bow Street 'beak.' I have only tried to sketch three or four of the most earnest readers, and I must leave you to exercise your own powers of observation upon the rest.

H. S. L.

UPSTAIRS AND DOWN.

By Jack Easel.

IF I were asked what leading feature of our domestic economy would be most likely to attract the attention of an intelligent foreigner, on his first visit to the metropolis, I should unhesitatingly answer — area railings. We sons and daughters of perfidious Albion (or of Merry England, if you like it better), can hardly realize to ourselves the sense of extreme novelty which Mossoo must experience at finding himself in a city where he is contemned to walk or drive through endless groves of iron. Turn in what direction he will through habitable London, whether within the dingy, but eminently fashionable purlieus of Mayfair, the spick-and-span new district of Tyburnia, Belgravia the aristocratic, Bloomsbury the respectable, Barnsbury the genteel, Clapham, Peckham, Fulham, Brompton, Hoxton, Brixton, Islington, Kensington, Kennington, — north, south, east, or west—his observant eye will rest on an interminable row of cast-iron spikes. The fact in itself is not a pleasant one to contemplate; and when Mossoo finds out that, behind these grim emblems of war, cellars are dug to a depth of some ten or twelve feet from the pavement level, in which cellars at least half the inhabitants of every house pass the greater part of their time, can't you imagine how he shrugs his shoulders, and opens his eyes with astonishment? But is it true, then, of these English, that they burrow in the ground for habitation, and condemn their domestics to reside in those *oubliettes* there? Parbleu! what a fate! Yes; it is even so; and Mossoo knows very well that honest Jules, who brushes his clothes at home, or Babet, who, with nothing on her head but a snow-white cap, frilled to a nicety, takes his children out for a walk in the Champs Elysées—either of these good creatures, I say, would grumble roundly, even if they didn't altogether pine away under such an infliction. Whereas Sairey-Jane, who comes up from her father's cottage on Dartmoor, with a pair of rosy cheeks and a strong Devonshire accent, accommodates herself kindly to her new situation—say that of deputy sub-assistant under scullery-maid, at eight pounds a year and her beer; gives up the green turf and purple heather of her native soil, for the prospect of a dull brick wall and coal-cellar door, only enlivened by the hasty glimpse which she gets of the lower halves of passing crinolines, and of peripatetic boots and trousers, worn by people who, from the knee upwards, are invisible to her. This is Sairey-Jane's fate, and that of master Tom, the page, who perhaps had the run of an orchard before he bloomed into buttons; though, to be sure, he does answer the front-door bell sometimes, and even goes out for an airing exactly three paces behind his 'missus,' which is so far an advantage to him.

I wonder how many of the upper ten thousand—those who live at the top, instead of the bottom of the kitchen-stairs—try to realize the effect of this semi-subterraneous existence; and which of us who are placed in authority over servants; who say to one 'do this,' and he doeth it (or doesn't do it, as the case may be)—which of us has explored, even in imagination, those gloomy labyrinths of the basement story? We are separated by, say twelve inches of floor carpentry, from a little world of beings possessed of the same physical and moral sense as ourselves; with desires, hopes, fears, and digestions like our own, and we take no more count of these last than we do of the works of a watch. The use of a watch is to tell us the time; but as for the mainspring, the lever action, the double escapement, the wheels and chain, or what you will, inside, do you, my dear lady, ever trouble your head one whit regarding them? Of course not. How should they concern you? Some chronometers —like that of your medical man, for instance—are made for use; others, like that of the pretty trinket at your waist, for ornament chiefly. So long as each serves its turn, neither you nor Dr. Glibb, I think, will meddle with its interior. Similarly, honest John Thomas, of Bellevue Cottage, Hammersmith, who is coachman, groom, and gardener by turn, has evidently been destined by nature to make himself generally useful; while Mr. Chawles Plushington, who stands airing his calves under a certain porch in Eaton Square, may be regarded as a purely ornamental feature in your establishment. All this is the result of fate. But the private disposition of these gentlemen, the quality of their respective temperaments, the number of their brothers and sisters, and, in short, their individual relations out of livery—are details which, confess now, have no interest for your ladyship. Indeed, in our present advanced and highly enlightened state of civilization it would be unreasonable to expect otherwise. But, as a pure matter of speculation, has it ever occurred to you what these humble retainers think of you? whether they may, perchance, have over the kitchen-fire, discussed your merits as a wife, a mother, the mistress of a household? The notion is an extravagant one, I admit, fraught with danger to, and subversive of the first interests of good SOCIETY; but, nevertheless, not altogether impossible. You remember, no doubt, that amusing story of your nursery days about a certain Palace of Truth, in which whoever spoke was, by an irresistible impulse, compelled to say just what he or she thought, neither more nor less. Conceive for an instant the effect of such an influence down-stairs and in your presence. What would they say?—good gracious! what might they not presume to say?—those cotton-velvet and bombazine-clad servitors, about those in authority over them—about you and me, for instance!

Place-aux-dames! Let us take the ladies first. There is Maria, your own maid, who, for a wage of some eighteen pounds a year, laces your corset, does your back-hair, selects your ball-dress (taking care, of course, that you don't appear twice during the season before the same people in the same costume), alters your bonnets of February to suit the requirements of March, and insists on your ordering another befitting the month of April; who brings that fragrant cup of tea to your bedside every morning; who knows where you keep the sal-volatile and kalydor, and with whom you condescend to chat a little as she unrobes you at three A.M. twice a week during the season. Ah! dear, good, patient Maria! sweet-spoken and sandy-haired sycophant! cease your kindly prattle about ribbons and bandoline, frizettes, Valenciennes, and sansflectum jupons, and tell your mistress what you really think of her. She is young, pretty, and engaging: will you dare to say she is a giddy and affected flirt? She is middle-aged, wealthy, and well-born: but have you ever called her a patched-up, imperious, skinflint? I trow not. The smile with which you greet her has been assumed so long, and with such excellent effect; that rising indignation has been so studiously repressed; that unimpassioned deference has told so well in regard to vails and perquisites—that I sometimes fancy you deceive yourself among the rest of the world, and, for the time, actually imagine the middle-aged lady whom you make up for evening-parties, and take to pieces at two P.M., is a model of feminine perfection. Women, you see, are born actors: their most effective arts are so natural to them; their simplest natures often so graceful and artistic, that, from the humblest servant-maid to the most accomplished lady of the land, we can't easily distinguish, I believe, that it might not be always desirable to distinguish between what they really are and what they seem to be. In point of fact, I don't think they always know themselves.

But trusty John Thomas, and profusely-powdered Chawles, only hide their spleen, their indignation and contempt, in the presence of their betters. In the butler's pantry, at the ale-house round the corner, across the hammer-cloths of their respective chariots—sentiments are expressed which neither you nor I, dear Paterfamilias, could listen to unmoved. I know an old gentleman—an irascible old gentleman—who, standing by chance one afternoon inconveniently near the top of the kitchen-stairs, after summoning his brougham for the second time that day, heard a favourite footman exclaim to the confidential valet, 'I'm blest if that infernal old noosance ain't ordered out the carriage again!'

Now you know that was by no means a pleasant remark to reach one's ears in the decline of life, uttered by a paid lacquey, the buttons of whose very coat were adorned with the family crest; but I am not at all sure that the old gentleman to whom I refer was justified in the severe retaliation which he adopted. The wretched Jenkins (let us call him) was dismissed on the spot, and had nothing but a month's wages to console him in his adversity. The consequence was, no doubt, that he repaired to the Black Lion that evening, and entertained his liveried friends with a very disrespectful, if not perverted account of the affair. I dare say his late master became the laughing-stock of the bar-parlour; that his wig and wizen face, his gout and gaiters, his peppery disposition and general peculiarities were discussed in a manner which was anything but pleasant. Suppose, instead of taking so summary a revenge, he had retired to his study, swallowed a glass of Madeira, just to steady his nerves, rung the bell, and told Jenkins not to talk so loud down-stairs if he wished to keep his place. Can't you imagine how crestfallen the poor minion would have been? what an old trump the man he served must thenceforth be considered in his eyes; and with how much zeal he might have continued his service? But, 'who can be wise, amazed, temperate, and furious,' as the Thane of Cawdor once justly asked, 'in a moment?' No man. And upon my word, when one comes to think of it, the provocation was very great.

Personally, I must admit I have no great affection for the London flunkey of fashionable life. It is the most unfortunate stage of a man-servant's career. As a page he may be slim and interesting. As a butler he may become stout and benevolent. But a great, broad-shouldered, black-whiskered fellow of six feet, who thrusts his brawny calves into pink silk stockings, plasters his hair with flour and pomatum, and covers himself with tags and gold lace, to hang on behind a carriage—bah! one fancies a man was made for some better business than this. It isn't his fault, no doubt, you will say. It is his betters who are to blame: they rig him up in this ridiculous costume; they set him to do this senseless work; they conduct their households on such a plan that it is difficult for him to help being what he is—mean, idle, often insolent. There are, in short, some excuses for him. And so, no doubt, a good deal might be said in favour of the wasp (black and yellow, by-the-way, is the orthodox colour for modern livery waistcoats), but that would not lessen the annoyance of its sting. Your ornamental footman is an institution: but the institution is a bore, and it is not exactly easy to say why it has become so. Any of us who have conned over, or seen enacted the comedies which were written at the close of the last century, can testify to the pleasant, affable character which the stage servant of that period assumed. His master joked with him, thrashed him, confided in him, called him 'knave' and 'rascal' by turns; and yet the poor fellow not only remained in his place, but stuck by the gallant captain through thick and thin; helped him in his little intrigues, bamfoozled his creditors, rushed into all sorts of risks for his sake. Can this be said of any of our liveried retainers of the present day? Can we imagine Jeames or Chawles convey-

ing a *billet-doux*, with the slightest interest as to its success? standing meekly to receive our blows (clouded canes are gone out of fashion now)? scheming to get a dun out of the house; or even remaining a single day beneath the roof of a gentleman in urgent pecuniary difficulties? I say that type of retainer is obsolete. You can no more find it now than you can find a living specimen of the dinornis or megatherium. What! confide our *tendresses* to a fellow who blacks one's boots?—talk familiarly about debts and obligations to a man who stands behind your chair at dinner? Impossible! Why the very next morning he would take you by the button-hole and call you 'old cove.' The present state of society no longer admits of such relations.

Women, I expect, do occasionally lapse into confidences of this kind. How otherwise could Miss Gadabout, with whose family I am tolerably intimate, have been informed of the fact that Lady Flaring has not paid her milliner's bill for the last three years; or that Cornet Spanker, of the Blues, had been twice refused by the wealthy widow, Mrs. McChequers? These little scraps of domestic intelligence are surely picked up on the second floor, before the toilet-table, between lacing and bandolining, late nocturnal soup and early morning Pekoe. Ah! ladies, ladies! if you would only be a *little* more discreet with your waiting-maids! If you would only remember that that dapper little creature who 'does' your back-hair, lugs out your ball-dress, selects your bracelets, ties your sash, twitches that bewitching skirt into shape, hands you your gloves, and scents that little scrap of cambric and lace which you carry with such a fascinating air – if you could only bring yourself to believe that your patient, useful, clever Abigail is— as great a gossip as yourself; that the harmless prattle with which you entertain her and indulge yourself, will assuredly find its way downstairs into the servants'-hall, and be carried next day to the dainty ears of a dozen of your female friends (or enemies, as the case may be)— would you—could you be *quite* so frank in your revelations? Miss Papyllon *is* a flirt, I grant you, and the manner in which she comported herself the other night before Lord Rattlegate was very far from correct. I am quite of your opinion, that, looking to Lady Screwby's position in the world, and the amount of her fortune, she ought *not* to wear cleaned gloves. But then, my dear girls, if every detail of *your* conduct last season—if all the sacred mysteries of *your* toilet were openly

1. Onions! – 2. a goose! – 3. sage! 4. a gander!!
AR   5. Some more onions –

discussed—which of the fairest of you would escape censure? I say nothing of Major Slingsby's attention to Miss Markham; nor of Miss Turnwell's amber-coloured silk *jupe*, over which that stupid footman spilt a strawberry ice last season, and which at least *some* of you recognised under a different hue this winter. I pass no comment on these things myself; I only beg of you to bear them in mind, and not to forget that what is sauce for the goose is also sauce for the gander— although I am aware that those delicious birds are not of the same sex.

It may be a morbid kind of curiosity, if you will, but I confess I do feel somewhat curious to know what forms the staple article of conversation round the kitchen-table; whether there is any standard of etiquette which regulates the social relations of this basement-story life; how much deference, for example, Mrs. Cook expects from the scullery-maid; what sort of attentions the parlour-maid may, with a due sense of propriety, receive from the butler; whether the valet patronises or only tolerates the page, and so forth. I fancy that servants in a well-conducted household are great sticklers for decorum and the fitness of things in general. Observe the nice distinctions which they draw with regard to their respective duties, settling among themselves, by an inevitable code of rules, who is to do what work. If by accident, or in case of emergency, the housemaid is asked to wash down the doorstep, cook to lend a hand at bed-making, or John to dust his master's library, ten to one you hear of grumbling, and a talk of this or that not being his or her 'dooty.' So we may depend on it the social grades of life downstairs are jealously preserved, that the nurserymaid knows herself (as the phrase goes) better than to trespass on the prerogative of my lady's attendant, and the 'buttons' wouldn't go for to interfere with Mr. John Thomas's perquisites, no not for nothink.

Perquisites! Ah! then we come to a point on which I think there should be some better understanding between 'upstairs and down.' When I was a student at the Royal Academy, with a moderate allowance from the parental purse, I used to spend my Easter week at a friend's house in the country, where an establishment was kept on rather a large scale. My railway journey there and back, cab fares, and other little incidental expenses cost me on those occasions perhaps somewhat more than I was justified in spending on such an excursion. But on leaving the house a tax awaited me which I really could not afford to pay, and yet from which no young gentleman with any sense of dignity could escape. My friend had a solemn butler—but of livery of course—with a bald head and an air of such tremendous importance that one instinctively felt (at least I did) how delicate a task it was to offer him any gratuity at all, and how utterly impossible it would have been to offer him anything less than gold without positively insulting him. The same argument applied with equal reason to the housekeeper, a demure-looking personage, who had breakfast served in her own room, and whom the other servants addressed as 'mum.' Then there was my friend's valet, who condescended to bring me my shaving-water in the morning and laid out my dress-coat before dinner. There was another gentleman in livery who during that repast came frequently to me with offers of a 'little sherry, sir, little 'ock, sir,' and so forth. Finally there were the groom who brought round our horses to the door, the gardener who had always some trifle to offer in the shape of fruit or vegetables as I was leaving (no doubt they thought, or pretended to think, that I had a house and *cuisine* of my own in town, whereas I lived in Bloomsbury lodgings, and my usual dinner consisted of a couple of chops), an I the lodge-keeper, who touched his hat whenever I entered or left the grounds. All these functionaries had, in turn, to be fee'd, and by the time their vails had been duly dispensed I was generally minus the best half of my last 5*l*. note. Now it seems to me that this system of servant-tipping requires revision. It falls rather hard on our young friends and poor relations—guests whose purses are slender—whose wallets are not amply stored. It makes John Thomas (whose calling, as I have shown, has from other causes already degenerated) mean and calculating; it leads him to look askance at every visitor to his master's house, and calculate his welcome in £. *s*. *d*. There is M'Chroner's housemaid, for instance, who used to smile and drop me the neatest little curtsies you ever saw whenever I called on her master. The angelic behaviour of that girl, the modest neatness of her white aprons, the tidy coquetry of her caps, the arch simplicity of her manner—she was only seventeen—completely won my heart. I don't mind admitting it now, for she has been married for some years to the grocer's young man, and they have since set up in that line for themselves. Well, in an evil moment I—don't be frightened, ladies, I have the very strictest sense of propriety—I took to giving this young woman small gratuities, for example, when she occasionally helped me on with my great-coat, half a crown; when she called a cab for me, half a crown; when she took charge of my Scotch terrier in the kitchen one morning (Mrs. Mac couldn't bear dogs), two-and-six, and so forth. One day my host found me out in my well-meant indiscretion, and being of an eccentric turn of humour, rated me in his own ironical way. 'My dear fellow,' said he, 'don't let me see you do that again. I pay that girl ample wages; if they are not high enough she can ask for more, and if she deserves 'em she shall have 'em. But meanwhile I don't see why, as my guest, you should requite her for my hospitality, such as it is. If that half-crown is an acknowledgment for the dinner which you have just eaten, *meis sumptibus*, give it to me and not to my housemaid. If

you think your entertainment here deserves some recognition at your hands, present me, at the close of every year, with a gold pencil-case, or what you will. Personally, I should hardly have considered that any such *honorarium* was necessary, but if it must be given, it is clearly I who should be the recipient.'

The result of this tremendous chaff (the drift of which I well understood, for M'Chromer's own generosity knew no bounds) was that Miss Susan's half-crowns were cut off, at least as far as I was concerned. Except at Christmas—which, you know, only comes once a year, and, regarded purely from a financial point of view, once is quite enough, in my opinion—that bewitching creature did not add sixpence more to her wages out of my pockets. It may have been owing to her master's cruel interference with her perquisites in this and other instances that she united herself at a month's warning with Mr. Spicely; or it may have been that youth's ardent devotion which caused her to take so precipitate a step. On that point it is not necessary for me to record an opinion. All I know is that I had from that day forth no more smiles, no more curtsies, no more inquiries after the health of my Skye terrier. I called my own cabs, pulled on my own great-coat, shut the front door in Gower Street with my own hands, and have been very suspicious of ancillary blandishments ever since.

There are two sides, however, to every question, and lest I should for an instant be supposed to defend stinginess to servants, let me here protest that I consider no kind of shabbiness more mean, no frugality more ill advised, no providence more wasteful than that which in any household is enjoined alone downstairs. 'A fat kitchen and a lean parlour' was a homely proverb once in vogue, and certainly if both cannot be well fed it must be a miserable sort of thriftiness which would begin by starving the basement story. Yet I have heard of respectable, well-bred housewives who ration their servants like union paupers, who cut down their daily food to a minimum, who consider a half-pint of small beer an amply-sufficient stimulant for an able-bodied, hard-working cook, and who regard the bare mention of meat suppers in the kitchen as flat heresy. There is something half-ludicrous, half-contemptible in this penny-wise economy. Upstairs and before her guests we have madame doing the honours of her table — a table crowded with needless delicacies— soups, entremets, game, pâtés, dessert, delicately-named wines (I say nothing of the quality), and what not. Could we foresee our hostess as she will probably appear next morning, marshalling the fragments of this gorgeous banquet in her bleak larder, taking stock of half-consumed chicken and segments of raised pie, counting the forcemeat-balls which adorned that dish of jugged hare, noting with a scrupulous eye the mortal remains of a beloved turkey, which of us would enjoy his dinner? Such relics may indeed worthily supply the family table for some days to come, but while all this feasting has been going on upstairs, how have the servants fared? 'What! *that* all of the shoulder of mutton which was ordered a week ago? Impossible! Those custards eaten because they wouldn't keep another day? Absurd! I am convinced that a *whole* leg of pheasant, and *not* a drumstick only, was sent down last night, and what presumption to eat game in the kitchen!' Ah, my dear Materfamilias, would you muzzle the ox that treadeth out the corn? Enough may not be always as good as a feast, but let us at least have enough in the servants' hall before we attempt feasting in the dining-room. The reverse of this rule represents not only a moral wrong but a financial mistake. Hungry servants must eat, whether they confess to the weakness or not. A good slice off the joint will satisfy their appetites as well as a series of oyster-patties, but if they are debarred from the first, can you be surprised at their making free with the other? Good servants, who wish (in downstair language) to 'better themselves,' and who want a fair character for their next place, never remonstrate with these petty exactions. Besides, the icy reserve and conventional propriety which is kept up (perhaps necessarily in this country) between man and master, maid and mistress, make it impossible to do so openly. But if this traditional gag were just for a day removed from the lips of honest John Thomas and Betsey Jane, my goodness! what a shout of derision would rise from the areas of Mayfair, with what loud bursts of vulgar indignation Belgravian basements would ring! I remember a famous back number of 'Punch,' in which there appeared, I think from the vigorous pencil of Leech, a sketch of some middle-aged nobleman who, thrusting his head out of a natty little brougham in an April shower, ordered his coachman and footman to give him their hats inside immediately, because they were new and would be spoiled by the rain. People laughed at this caricature, and accepting the spirit of the satire, no doubt put down the incident itself as a pure invention. It may indeed have been so, but not long afterwards I heard the following anecdote from a friend on whose accuracy I can rely, and I should not be surprised if the sketch and the story had some common and substantial origin.

The head of an illustrious house, whom I shall call Lord Skinflint, had given one of his cast-off hats to a certain lacquey in his service. Recognizing this hat a few days afterwards on the hall-table, where it had been left for the moment, my lord inquired to whom it belonged, and was at once reminded of his gift.

'What!' cried his lordship, 'did I give you such a good hat as this?'

The man explained that he had had it relined and 'done up.'

'Umph!' says my lord, 'I never thought of that. Pray, what did you pay for it?'

'Arf-a-crown, my lord,' answers Mr. Jeames.

The nobleman mused for an instant, and looked at the hat again. 'I'll tell you what,' said he, at length, 'I'll give you five shillings for it as it is.'

'If your lordship pleases,' answered the footman. (In fact there was nothing else for him to say.)

The bargain was struck at once. Lord Skinflint put on the hat, and, for aught I know, he may wear it still.

Well, I won't moralize on this story, for despite my friend's proverbial accuracy, it is just possible that he may have been misinformed; that the anecdote is what the Italians call *ben trovato*, or, in plain English, that there is not a single word of truth in it. But I confess that to me it does not seem so highly improbable, and, I will candidly add, similar gossip has led me to believe that there is not unfrequently in 'high life' a great deal that might be contemplated with advantage by philosophers below stairs. Do the philosophers avail themselves of this teaching? I fear not. Jeames and Chawles, Susan and Betty imitate the foibles no less than the virtues of their betters. We all admit and deplore that spirit of flunkeydom which pervades certain phases of English Society, which sets half our dear fellow-countrymen truckling to a man who has a handle to his name, or, worse still, to another who is known to possess a large fortune. After this can you sneer at the mixture of sham deference and twopenny dignity of the servant who wears, for your sake, a cockade, tags, powder, and heraldic buttons? I think it is a mistake to suppose that servants despise and groan under these insignia of office. My own opinion is, that if livery went out of fashion for footmen, butlers would at once petition to wear it. A due and palpable distinction between the two places must be kept up, or the kitchen would be in a state of anarchy. What! a drab coat or a striped vest the badge of slavery? The badge of fiddlesticks! A domestic servant is not more rigidly tied to his duties than a soldier, or a government-office clerk, or a barrister, or a poor curate, who is often harder worked than a London footman, and not nearly so well remunerated. We don't call a red jacket, or a tie-wig, or a stuff gown the badge of slavery: why should an honest suit of livery be so stigmatized? Prate as they will about their free-born rights and privileges, servants are the first to respect these relics of ancient feudalism. Not long ago a cook who was out of a situation asked a lady to assist her in getting one. Before long, a place was found, and a consultation held on the subject.

'Pray mum,' asked Mrs. Cook, 'does the family 'ave *cresses*?'

'Water-cresses for breakfast? I'm sure I don't know,' answered her kind patron, 'but what can it signify?'

'*Excuse* me, mum,' interposed the applicant, 'I don't think I make myself understood. *I* mean cresses on their carriage, note-paper, liv'ry, and ceterer—'

'Oh! armorial bearings, you mean?' said the lady. 'I really cannot tell you.'

'Because 'm, I reely couldn't undertake a situation where there wasn't a cross kept. You see, ev'ry genteel fam'ly 'as a cross; and——'

'And you positively make that a condition?' asked the lady, quietly.

'Sutt'nly, mum,' says Mrs. Cook. 'Footman kep; washing put out; beer, tea, and fam'ly cross.'

'Then, I really think, Mrs. Cullender,' said the lady, smiling, 'that you had better look out for yourself. John, show this silly woman to the door.'

he Market Assistant: Containing a brief Description of every Article of Human Food sold in the Public Markets of the cities of New York, Boston, Philadelphia, and Brooklyn; including the various Domestic and Wild Animals, Poultry, Game, Fish, Vegetables, Fruits, etc., etc., with many curious incidents and anecdotes. By THOMAS F. DE VOE, author of the "Market Book," etc. With numerous explanatory illustrations. One vol. 8vo. Price $2.50.

"It is a practical market assistant to the careful housewife or head of a family gaged in the consideration of the question, 'What shall we hav for dinner?' d is at the same time a magazine of curious and interesting historical facts, ecdotes, and incidents attractive to the general reader." — *Cleveland Herald.*

wo Thousand Miles on Horseback. Santa Fé and Back: a Summer Tour through Kansas, Nebraska, Colorado, and New Mexico, in the year 1866. By Colonel JAS. F. MELINE. One vol. crown 8vo. Price $2.00.

"He is a good traveller, and, combining the disciplined mind of a student ith the training of an army officer, is well qualified to give an opinion upon hat he observes. His mode of travelling has furnished him with excellent portunities for careful observation, and with great variety of adventure in the airie." — *New Bedford Standard.*

"It is a lively, descriptive history of the country passed through, imparting uch valuable information, and makes a capital companion to the 'Across the ontinent,' and other books of inter-continental travel of the past few years." — *'oston Commonwealth.*

'our Years among the Spanish-Americans. By Hon. F. HASSAUREK. late U. S. Minister Resident to the Republic of Ecuador. One vol. crown 8vo. Price $2.00.

"The subject is full of interest, and we commend the volume to our readers one of the best of the year for information." — *Hartford Press.*

talian Journeys. By WILLIAM D. HOWELLS, Author of "Venetian Life." One vol. crown 8vo. Price $2.00.

"Seldom a writer makes so broad and fine a mark with his first pen-stroke Mr. Howells, our late accomplished Consul at Venice, made with his 'Venean Life.' The critics found so much to praise in this book that for once they rgot their avocation, and paused to admire and enjoy, instead of hastening to int out the defects and faults." — *Liberal Christian.*

"Since the days of Montaigne and Lord Herbert of Cherbury (not to menon James Howell again), no traveller in Italy has written more entertaining counts of his journey than our countryman, Mr. Howells, whose 'Venetian ife' we noticed some months ago." — *Boston Commonwealth.*

'enetian Life. By WILLIAM D. HOWELLS. One vol. crown 8vo. Price $2.00.

"It is really very delightful to get hold of a book that tells us so much of culiar national life, habit, and character, in such a charming style. Generally avellers have so much of the gorgeous architecture that they forget to tell us hat the people eat, drink, and wear, and how they live withal." — *Milwaukee Visconsin.*

he Turk and the Greek; or, Creeds, Races, Society, and Scenery in Turkey, Greece, and the Isles of Greece. By S. G. W. BENJAMIN. One vol. 16mo. Price $1.75.

"If anybody wishes a small volume of facile, graceful, mobile prose, we comend him to these rather miscellaneous yet entertaining pages." — *New York ndependent.*

"The style of this book is that of an easy narrative; the sympathies are those f a right-minded American; and the predictions are shared in common with telligent observers everywhere." — *Brooklyn Union.*

"The author's account of Greece is not flattering, but no doubt it is true." — *altimore Episcopal Methodist.*

HURD AND HOUGHTON'S
EDITIONS OF
DICKENS'S WORKS.

THE RIVERSIDE DICKENS!
Why it is the Best Library Edition.

1. The English Illustrations by Cruikshank, Phiz, Seymour, Leech, and others, are all *newly engraved* on steel, from early impressions, in exact *fac-simile* of the originals, and are not like other editions printed from old worn-out plates.
2. It contains all the *superb designs* of F. O. C. Darley and John Gilbert, which, being copyright, cannot be used in the editions of other publishers.
3. It is printed on fine paper, with wide margins, allowing room for the largest engravings, which are not injured in trimming the volumes, as often occurs in other editions.
4. The engravings are all on steel, and no wood cuts are used, as in other editions, thus giving uniformity together with more beautiful illustrations.

The Publishers invite a comparison of the "Riverside Edition" of Dickens's Works with other editions.

Price in cloth, cut or uncut edges, $2.50; in half calf, $4.00.

There are now issued:

OLIVER TWIST, 1 vol.
MARTIN CHUZZLEWIT, 2 vols.
OLD CURIOSITY SHOP, 2 vols.
NICHOLAS NICKLEBY, 2 vols.
CHRISTMAS STORIES, 1 vol.
BARNABY RUDGE, 2 vols.
DOMBEY AND SON, 2 vols.

THE GLOBE DICKENS!
Why it is the Best Cheap Edition.

1. It is handsomely printed upon fine white paper, from large, clear types, and is the most legible cheap edition in the market.
2. It contains all the designs of F. O. C. Darley, the foremost American designer, and John Gilbert, the foremost English designer, all engraved on steel in the best manner. These designs being copyright, cannot be used by other publishers.
3. Each work is comprised in a single volume, and the whole of Dickens's Works in thirteen volumes, at $1.50 per volume. The set complete, $19.50; half calf, $39.00.

"But none of the Dickens series are now selling so freely as Hurd & Houghton's 'Globe.' Its generous type and clear print and low price combined make it very popular, and the printers cannot keep up with the demand." — *Springfield Republican.*

THE HOUSEHOLD DICKENS!
A Favorite Edition.

In fifty-three volumes, 16mo, containing all the choice designs of Darley and Gilbert. Price, cloth, $1.25 per volume. The set, cloth, $66.25; half calf, $132.50.

HURD AND HOUGHTON'S
LIBRARY OF CHOICE FICTION.

No. 1. Playing for High Stakes. By ANNIE THOMAS. With illustrations. 1 volume 8vo, paper. Price, 50 cents.

No. 2. Beautiful Miss Johnson, and other Stories. With illustrations. 1 volume 8vo, paper. Price, 50 cents.

No. 3. Sketches of Society and Travel. By an Amateur Casual and others. With illustrations. 1 volume 8vo, paper. Price, 50 cents.

No. 4. Mary Egglestone's Lover, and other Tales. With illustrations. 1 volume 8vo, paper. Price, 50 cents. (Nearly ready.)

No. 5. Sketches of Club-Life, Hunting, and Sports. With illustrations. 1 volume 8vo, paper. Price, 50 cents. (Nearly ready.)

HURD AND HOUGHTON, Publishers,
459 BROOME STREET, NEW YORK.

*** These works are for sale by all booksellers and news agents.

www.ingramcontent.com/pod-product-compliance
Lightning Source LLC
Chambersburg PA
CBHW020119170426
43199CB00009B/566